What Is Cool?

What Is Cool?

Understanding Black Manhood in America

Marlene Kim Connor

Crown Publishers, Inc.
New York

The author gratefully acknowledges permission to reprint the following:

"We're a Winner" (Curtis Mayfield), © 1967 Warner-Tamberlane Publishing Corp. All rights reserved. Used by permission.

"The Gender Divide," reprinted by permission of The Wall Street Journal, © 1994 Dow Jones Company, Inc. Rights reserved worldwide.

Published by Crown Publishers, Inc., 201 East 50th Street, New York, New York 10022. Member of the Crown Publishing Group.

Random House, Inc. New York, Toronto, London, Sydney, Auckland

CROWN is a trademark of Crown Publishers, Inc.

Manufactured in the United States of America

Design by Linda Kocur

Library of Congress Cataloging-in-Publication Data

Connor, Marlene Kim.
What is cool?: Understanding Black manhood in America / by Marlene Kim Connor.—1st ed.
1. African-American men. I. Title.
E185.86.C584   1995
305.38'89073—dc20   94-44038

ISBN 0-517-79965-0

1   3   5   7   9   10   8   6   4   2

First Edition

To my mother, Cleo Connor,

a really special lady who,

when some guy zipped his car

into a parking space

she was waiting to back in to

(a hanging offense in New York City),

totally lost her cool and shouted

with all the venom she could muster,

"I hope you have a very bad day!"

Acknowledgments

most of us don't get a chance to thank people for all the world to see, so I am going to take this opportunity to its absolute max.

I want to thank my mother, Mamie Cleo Connor, who unfortunately passed away a few years before this book could be published. She was the most dynamic, caring, and determined lady in the world. She always wanted us to succeed, but to be *different*. I love her deeply, and will for all time.

Thank you, Dad, Cecil L. Connor, for always supporting my talents and ideas, for always listening, for making the commitment to being a good father no matter what it took, and for being strong enough as a man to be patient, and kind.

Thanks to my sister, Deborah Connor Coker (who is also an author, of children's books), for being the arbiter of cool throughout my life ("He ain't cool"; "Look, he thinks he's cool"; "He'd be a lot better off if he wasn't trying so hard to be cool"). She never has anointed anyone as truly cool, which tells you a lot about how elusive it is, and about how women perceive it.

I must thank Carol Taylor, my editor, who knocked me out when she expressed her enthusiasm for my writing and my theories. Everyone should be blessed with an editor who is so supportive, so talented, and so very, very good at what she does.

Thanks also to the rest of the Crown family, including Betty A. Prashker, who blew me away when she sat next to me at a luncheon and told me I could write and how much she enjoyed this book, and Jo Fagan, who was always cool with me when we worked together.

I have to say a special thanks to Professor James Miller at Trinity College in Harford, Connecticut, for allowing me to explore cool for my thesis when I was an undergrad, and for providing so much insight and direction throughout my college days. And to Marie Brown, for picking up that ball early on in this book's development and supporting this idea the minute she read it.

Thanks to Terry Williams for his immediate support and endorsement. And thanks, Gylbert Coker, for all your help.

Thanks to Dean Charles B. Watkins and the other folks at the School of Engineering at the City College of New York for their support and friendship.

Thanks to Violet Carter, assistant principal, and David LeDay, both of Edison High School in Minneapolis; and thanks to Lafayette Mikals of North High School for getting doors opened to me so quickly. Also, thanks to all those stimulating and interesting young people who talked with me.

Thank you, Marc Lippman, King Downing, Walter Braswell, Rick Sampson, Steve Williams, Frank Borges, Archie Colander, Douglas Macaulay, Sterling and Greg Reese, Nat Williams, Carlos Rodriguez, Ronnie Brown, Myles and Pete Coker, Jay Wesley, Jim Sumler, Jack Barthwell, Steve Brereton, Eugene Burke, Kermit Stamper, Benny, Allan, and Junior Lorick, my cousin Robert "Chuck" Rhue, Harry, and Lamar for being truly cool black men and for letting me observe you throughout my life.

Oh, and for the same reason, I must also thank Curtis Mayfield, Marvin Gaye, Gil Scott-Heron, members of Earth, Wind & Fire, Malcolm X, Michael Jordan, Wesley Snipes, Richard Roundtree (although he should have told his woman he loved her when they were on the phone), Barry White, John Amos, Yaphet Kotto, Bryant Gumbel, Thurgood Marshall, Andrew Young, James Brown, Will Smith (although I liked the other mother better), Hubert Davis (for keeping his cool in game 5 and, when reporters asked how he stayed so cool, for responding, by "thinking of my father"), and hundreds of others.

I'd like to thank Edie, Beverly, Carla, Gene, and Shirley for being what friends should be.

And, finally, thank you so much, John, for being my hero.

Contents

Foreword

Once in awhile a book comes along that captures the public imagination and helps to define who we are and where we fit into the larger frame of reality. *What Is Cool?* does just that. We have heard such pejorative terms as the "X" and the "clueless" generation, referring to young people under twenty-five who are perceived to be confused about values, unclear about morals, and uncertain about their overall direction in life. Marlene Connor's book helps us see, through the medium of cool, a phenomenon we often hear about and even talk about in our everyday lives but seldom know what it really means.

The meaning of what is cool as it relates to Black manhood heretofore has been obscure, in part, because it is often concealed behind a shroud of idiosyncratic language, copy-cat imitation of gestures and changing moods.

Cool is the cousin to hip, but unlike hip, cool is not against everything mainstream, is not about total disaffection, nor does it resemble a total culture of refusal. Cool is an unexpected attitude catching the society off-guard and conquering defiantly with its own inimitable style. Connor gives us a quite different meaning, one that is more over-arching and profound. She posits a paradigm for understanding the way certain behavior is exhibited as it relates to Black manhood in this country. The important element here and about this book is that while it will be controversial it will also make us think about the creative ways Black men have found to control their rage in America. And it is this element of discipline that is the cornerstone to understanding cool. Connor points out that America does not understand the discipline it takes to withhold the rage and anger Black men feel in this country. And this control, played out through the medium of cool, should be seen as a highly valued virtue. Were it not for such restraint, she argues, our society would see much more of that rage expressed, not less, and not only brother against brother—but against the larger society.

In her chapter "Street Cool," culture is the pervasive concept and is played out, acted out in Black life mostly by teenagers through music, dance, language, and violence. Hip-hop, for instance, became the voice of defiance and reason in the 1980s for Black teenage males, and cool was the ungirdling for the medium. In America today, where everyone is hip but few are truly cool, what does it mean to really embody cool? What does it mean for men and women? The implacable cool is defined in all its nuances by Connor as she examines Black manhood while providing the flavor for understanding where we are in this society and how our children are affected and influenced by lifestyle.

In "Revolutionary Cool," the emphasis is on history and survival mostly beginning in the 1960s, when knowledge and intelligence were the keys to being cool. The suppression of emotions, anger, and resentment caused much of that inner turmoil to be projected onto those closest to them: their peers and Black women. This is in part because "talking back" to the "enemy" was, and is, problematic. But as a result of this lashing out some important questions about Black culture emerged.

What *is* Black culture? What are some of its aesthetic components? What is beauty? How is culture produced? What symbols and language should be used? What stories should be told? What rituals performed? Another important element in *What Is Cool?* is how Black culture both expresses and shapes the Black man's strategies in navigating their world. She hazards to say young Black males can resist defeat by "talking back" to the larger culture about racism and oppression through cool.

The need to "talk back" or act out became the way in the 1960s, when talking back was elevated to an art form and everybody did it. Talking back was the way Black leaders, teenagers, prisoners, women, and a host of others found voice to express their resentment about exclusion in the hope that they would be a part of the inclusion process. Connor makes the point that blacks developed psychological, physiognomic, and linguistic approaches to accommodate her paradigm of cool. On the psychological dimension the mandate was to reserve emotions, develop discipline, be defiant, yet survive. The physiognomic expression was to develop cultural ways of acting, mannerisms, walking (what Ellison once called the most elegant walk in the world). A handshake had to have a quality that set it apart. It had to come from "our" culture, not "theirs." Style became the way. Talking, for instance, involved complex uses of languages that removed qualifiers, enhanced verbs, rejected neutral words, and banished comparatives. The linguistic aspect of cool is aggression wrapped in sexual innuendo and is often used to express bravado and at times turn women into victims. But it was male talk reserved for males by males in exclusive domains: street corners, prisons, pool halls, bars, and clubs. This was cool. But it was only cool for a time, and for the men, not the women. But the men in Connor's model of cool never intended to have an audience mixed in race, class, and especially not gender.

All the best qualities of cool, according to Connor—élan, sincerity, violence, immediacy, tension—are lessened in a cool woman's world. Connor's chapter "Women and Cool" seems to consist, in a significant way, in avoiding conflict yet seeking the approval of their men. Women want to be cool too, as they must be, in order to get the men in a position to confront the ironies of cool. Connor makes a cogent point in the book when she writes, "Woman has always sought a man who can survive and who can conquer. And so, even in this day of civilized and sophisticated society, survivors and conquerors are considered the most desirable, the sexiest. In the inner city, the cool guys are the most sought after."

Cool does not lend itself to easy analysis, but the implications of "cool" as an important concept for urban Black youths rings true in the book. For the male, being cool is a layered process, and for the woman to dissect those layers she must gain his trust, show patience, and be strong. Since cool is tied to a system, largely rewarded and punished by a community of peers, a woman cannot completely strip all the nuances of being cool away. But she can persevere and often does to be with and for her man. Connor makes it clear that this is about relationships between men and women, between teenagers and adults, and between black people and their society. The ultimate test of cool for the woman is to accept the male as he is and not change him for all time but bifurcate him, split him up so he can become whole by adapting to white society, and raising his consciousness so he will see the enemy as not in his peers but without. The woman, according to Connor, should assist in making him adapt to the variety of worlds he encounters; white and black, uptown and downtown, the office and the street, the university and the " 'hood" social club. "Electronic Cool," the fourth chapter in Connor's work, is analogous in some respects to finding voices and heroes on radio in the 1950s but in the televised world of today. Today's cultural heroes, people like Arsenio Hall, Damon Wayans, Bill Cosby, Bobby Brown, and Queen Latifah, to name only five, exude cool and are fair game to be emulated and respected by black youth. But electronic cool is not only about stars or media images, but about money. "Cool was always a system created out of necessity and circumstance," Connor writes. "What was most disturbing was that an entire generation of young people for the first time were placed with white America's direct manipulation of cool through the media, aided by Blacks who wanted to get paid. It became cool to get paid, and therefore cool itself became a product."

By this time in Connor's book, cool is no longer willing to be regarded as street, or primitive or revolutionary, and now had to be cerebral, street, primitive, and revolutionary all in one. Enter "Middle-Class Cool."

Middle-class cool, in Connor's analysis, arose at an unexpected time because no one expected the middle class to ever be "cool." But many middle-class Blacks, like street cool folks, have been angry at white America and resented the assertion that they were "making it" not because of their own intelligence and hard work but because of some "affirmative action program." Middle-class teenagers and adults want to express, in lifestyle, the elements of cool. And many did. But since being cool is something "bestowed," middle-class Blacks were completely shut out of the authentic system of cool. They had to redefine the paradigm, or at least find an experiential side to express traditional cool within the original street model.

Young Black street males devised the system of cool to establish their own manhood rites in the face of dangers in their immediate ecological niche—the street. The traditional middle-class teenager was not considered cool by street definition. But two important events occurred that changed all that. The first was in the 1970s, when a new Black middle class was spawned composed of Blacks who were streetwise, and second, by the 1990s the attitude of street kids through television, radio-rap, on college campuses, and occasionally on the street. For middle-class kids the survival game was different but no less real. Connor points out that, "There was a *need* now to succeed, a *need* to pursue a career, and a need to function, but not necessarily in a white man's world." Cool became a spiritual guide. Cool kept one different and distinct from the oppressive other. Cool helped middle-class kids survive when they felt alone and isolated on sprawling campuses and engaging in a segregated social life.

Middle-class cool was indeed born out of an almost invisible despair and psychic loneliness and the professed desire to find a cultural anchor on an island of resentment—the college campus. Prior to that, cool was not necessary to get middle-class girls: being cool was considered uncouth by all middle-class codes of conduct. Cool was in its essence about the street and the kid on the block in the neighborhood and how to make it through the next day.

What Is Cool? is a woman's personal account of how Black

manhood is achieved in America. It is a view from the trenches by a person who has lived through the various levels of cool and found voice to express what she has seen and felt. Marlene Connor presents a fresh look at a powerful cultural legacy and writes masterfully about a generation of youth and what it means to be Black, young or old, wealthy or poor, in a difficult environment and survive against the odds.

Terry Williams, Ph.D.,
author of *The Uptown Kids:*
Struggle and Hope in the
Projects, and founder of
The Writers' Crew

By Webster's definition, cool in the real sense means:
"Lacking warmth; moderately cold."

Then Webster gets a little vague on us:
"Marked by steady, dispassionate calmness and self-control."

Then Webster gets a little bitter on us:
"Lacking ardor or friendliness."

And then Web gets closer to the truth:
"Marked by restrained emotion or excitement."

Being a *hipster* is having "very limited responses
to anything that happens."
—Wynton Marsalis
on *60 Minutes,* talking to a young Juilliard student

Introduction

Whenever I mention the subject of this book to anyone, I get the same response: "Great. Are you finally going to tell people what's cool and what isn't, who's cool and who isn't? Are you gonna tell us how to wear our sneakers, or how to hold a cigarette?" The word *cool* has been adopted into the mainstream as a term that describes anybody who marches to the beat of a different drummer, who blazes trails, who follows no trends, who is sexy, a loner, mysterious, hip, self-assured, different, quiet, confident, rebellious . . .

Well, cool is all of those things. But it is really something much more important than that. Cool is perhaps the most important force in the life of a Black man in America.

Now, I know that's a huge generalization and that it sounds like a rather ambitious notion. But after careful consideration, I think it's safe to make such a statement. *Cool is perhaps the most important force in the life of a Black man in America.* Cool is the closest thing to a religion for him, and it is easily his most basic method of determining manhood. It is a substitute for the rites of passage for a white male in this society, and for the rites of passage of the African warriors that Black boys once were before their days of captivity.

Cool is not just a term, it is a lifestyle. It has little to do with the hippest clothes or the latest fad. Cool became the new rules and new culture for those Black people who rejected white American culture and white America's notions of how people should behave. It became the new definition for manhood and maturity in a life that is devoid of certain tools and is abundant in others. The language is different, the symbols are different, and finally the men themselves are different.

To understand most of the Black men in this country, particularly the ones who seem to cause "America" the most trouble or who seem to refuse to accept its system, it is essential that you come to understand cool, because he lives by its dictates more than by the dictates of anything else. It is the most powerful yet intangible force in Black America. It is to be praised and at the same time it is insidious. The word to describe it might change from time to time, but its rules never do.

This book attempts to examine what cool really is, and why. I have tried to capture the essence and origins of this phenomenon. I have to admit that I have come to dislike the phenomenon of cool; in many instances, it no longer serves us well. But I know how important cool is, and has been, to the Black existence in this country. I hope after reading this, you will, too.

chapter one

Street Cool

"Street life,

it's the only life I know."

—The Crusaders, 1975

being Black in America is distinctly different from belonging to any other group of people. Black Americans have a history that is rich and unique, beginning with why we are in this country. We were brought to America as captives. *Captivity* is a much more accurate word than *slavery* because *slavery* implies to me a state of mind, a God-given status, a caste system determined at birth. Therefore, I've used *captives* in place of *slaves* throughout the text.

Black Americans are not immigrants or legal aliens. By virtue of our history we are Americans; easily as American as any European American. We also possess a kinship with the Native American because of our understanding of the dismantling of a culture.

3

Black Americans also hold another important distinction. We are the only people in this country whose identities are steeped mostly in the American culture. In the attempt to enslave them, the captives were stripped of their language, religion, rituals, rites, families, and weaponry. Their methods of communication, manner of dressing, and general lifestyle were destroyed. They had no kinship to one another because different tribes were deliberately placed together so that communication could not take place.

The Africans who were brought to this country were from many different tribes, spoke different languages, and probably did not share common religions. It is safe to say, however, that indigenous Africans were hunters, warriors, and farmers, and had a culture based on survival in the natural elements of their environment. Because slave traders were not interested in the feebleminded, the weak, or the thin, who might die during the trip across, or might not fetch them a hefty sum, they brought over the strongest and healthiest people whenever possible. While this displacement might have dismantled language and religious practices, it did not totally destroy physical strength, personal pride, and emotional fortitude. Instead it created a deep and potentially dangerous desire in these people to regain the strength and freedom they had once enjoyed, and more important it created a level of anger that cannot be measured.

Life after the middle passage was an irrational existence. The world of the captive African was filled with confusion, despair, and a lack of love, family, or anything familiar. After a bitter emotional war all that was left was to adopt and to conform to what at the time was white American language, religion, and behavior. Simply put, these captives had to learn the language and toil the land. Enslavement is successful when pride and strength are stripped away and are replaced with complacency, weakness, and acceptance of captivity. The real struggle with the African captive was a psychological one; the battlefield was the mind.

Slavery in this country was never a total success. These captives toiled the land, but they also systematically developed a new culture, a subculture, a Black African American culture. This new American culture was, at first, a combination of pride, lack of education, poverty, physical strength brought on by hard work and punishment, emotional strength fortified by determination and adaptation, and memories of a very different past, kept alive through the oral tradition.

For many, but not all, of these African Americans, this subculture was based on a hatred for, and a rejection of, all that was white American. This rejection of all that was white, and the unwillingness to define one's self according to the enemy's lifestyle, has remained for many an integral part of existence in this country ever since the captive experience, and in many ways is at the core of what has become not only street cool but street *life*.

While enslavement had not taken place in the souls of these captives, it is not realistic to imply that the African captive was not physically and emotionally powerless. With shackles on their ankles, whips to their backs, and the lack of an education that would have given them the skills to thrive in this new world, these Africans were indeed enslaved. The opportunity for unity was denied and the cultural tools that define and educate other American men did not exist; instead, confusion and despair took their place.

The loss of cultural mores is incredibly debilitating. Every culture defines its own survival needs and devises its own methods of determining strength and self-worth. With their tribal culture destroyed, there was a devastating loss of rituals and rites of passage with which to define and shape the male child and transform him from child to man. This loss threatened to render these fledgling African Americans culturally impotent.

The African captive was forced to learn and accept a definition of manhood that was vague and foreign to him and, as a captive, impossible for him to achieve. Not only were there few means by which a young boy could attain this new definition, but there was little desire to embrace this definition, for it was degrading to try to become the enemy. The white man demonstrated little about *his* manhood to admire; he achieved supremacy by enslaving others and potency by raping women. He seemed ruthless, money-hungry, and moral-less.

Not all captives experienced constant pain and degradation. There were many who were allowed to sustain families and meager households. But there were many more of these early African Americans who were forced to witness and endure an inhuman and inhumane existence and were subjected to worse if they reacted outwardly to it. Men whose systems of manhood were probably established through conquering their enemy or through demonstrating strength and prowess in the field were now punished swiftly and severely if they were caught showing anger or retaliating.

Therefore it became essential to survival itself for these early African American males to remain outwardly calm while watching their women raped and beaten, their sons, brothers, and fathers tortured, humiliated, or lynched for protecting themselves or for rebelling. They knew that if they reacted, punishment would be swift and brutal. Survival became both physical and mental, because death threatened both body and mind. The captives had to condition themselves to remain impassive, to mask their emotions, to internalize their anger.

Internalizing emotions became, for many African American males, their only means for survival. It is this internalization process that is the beginning of cool. Anger, love, happiness, hatred—these emotions were all potentially dangerous if expressed. Love meant certain disappointment and it left you emotionally vulnerable. An open display of hatred or even anger meant certain punishment. An open demonstration of happiness might mean the removal or destruction of whatever made you happy.

Natural emotions became repressed; this is one of the first characteristics of being cool. Irrevocably, repressed emotions will manifest themselves as depression and hypersensitivity. Subsequently it is no surprise that African Americans evolved into a very emotional race of people.

Although this history of captivity is familiar to most Americans, it is essential that we remember the experience in order to understand the desperate *need* people had to create a system that teaches emotional control from the minute a child begins to walk. *Need* is at the root of what makes cool—in its purest form—a uniquely Black experience. At the root of cool is the need for it. Some would argue that cool can be found in dozens of non–Black communities. True, there may be rules that dominate the male world of any subculture that have been labeled *cool*. But the word *cool* is really a description of a collective lifestyle, a code of behavior, that spoke very specifically to the Black experience, which evolved from a desperate need. And when cool changes, it changes out of need. Without the need, there is no cool.

During captivity, cool was in its infancy. Being cool meant surviving, at its most basic level. But after captivity, cool, as we recognize it today, began to take shape, responding to new circumstances and new needs. In the beginning that need was simply the *need to survive*. As time went on that need became the *need to define an achievable manhood*.

The much-awaited Emancipation in 1865 resulted in new and unforeseen obstacles. There were no jobs, no fine houses, no forty acres and a mule, no safety, no respect, nothing. Eventually the influx into the northern cities began, as Blacks arrived in search of work and in search of the promised land where whites treated them with respect.

Blacks now intermingled with whites as free men, and cohabited with other struggling Blacks. There became an even stronger need to protect oneself from one's own deeply rooted anger and fears. Life was no longer defined by bondage and by boundaries, and emotions ran high as northern and southern Blacks fought for jobs.

So out of *need*, cool became a system that served many purposes. At its initial core was survival—physical and emotional. Soon it would evolve into something much more complex, subtle, tangible, and important. You might ask, What's more important than physical survival? Well, as many Blacks will tell you, living as a Black man (or woman) with dignity, cultural and personal pride, and satisfaction is more important than simply surviving. In the renowned movie *The Liberation of L. B. Jones,* death liberated Mr. Jones. He *chose* to die rather than live as a financially successful Black man whose manhood was constantly being questioned—even by his wife, who told him that the redneck deputy was more man than L. B. would ever be. Jones suffered from one of America's oldest jokes: What do you call a Black doctor from Virginia? A nigger.

Black men were now expected, by their women, to become heads of the families. They had to become mature, responsible, providing men in a world where their ability to achieve "manhood" was previously nonexistent. Manhood and maturity come not just through the passing of time, but through emotional growth, self-esteem, responsibility, and a growing sense of one's ability to survive and provide for himself and his loved ones. The captive retained from his slavery experience nothing but degradation and a total lack of self-worth. This had to be combated. The early African Americans had to regain their pride if they were to survive as free people.

At this point, achieving manhood for a Black man was confusing and ill-defined. To be a *man* in America you had to adhere to the rules of the white man. But those rules did not apply to the Black man's life, and even when they did, adhering to those rules seemed to require a compromise few Black men were willing to make. America, a nation devoted to capitalism, defines manhood through achievement, money, possessions. Black men had very little money, and very few means of earning it. The Black man had to develop a reality for himself, a new culture that protected and empowered him within his own environment, his own neighborhood; a code of honor that conveyed his growing manhood, and eventually anointed him with the coveted title of "man." Eventually *cool* responded to that need, and became an unspoken code that taught a Black boy how to become a man, among his peers and in his environment. In America, if you do not create or possess wealth, power, or status—relative to your environment and peer group—you will not be deemed a "man." However, the rules of cool developed out of the unique struggles a Black male faces in the ghettos and on the streets of America's cities, miles away from the America of amber waves of grain. Slowly, cool, as we recognize it today, developed into a silent code of behavior, a lifestyle, a barometer, a measuring stick, a reality check, a method for determining when and if a Black boy has achieved "manhood." The tools and rules of cool were developed in a subculture of poverty and dis-education. Therefore, cool's rules toward manhood have little to do with America's rules toward manhood.

Many Black men today feel that America is threatened by and hostile toward a Black man even thinking himself a man unless he has achieved that status by America's standards. They feel that during captivity any attempt to become a man, by a Black man's definition, was always swiftly beaten down; attempting to flee captivity or raising one's voice or hand to protect his family received swift and often deadly punishment. It seems to them that America is still threatened by the possibility of a Black man seeing himself as a man, and to them, it is this sense of a "threat" that creates the Rodney King incident and verdict, the killing of Black leaders, the destruction by the media of Black men who rise to prominence, and on and on. Frankly, it does seem as though America is not only threatened by the Black man becoming a man, it is hostile toward him even thinking himself a man, unless he has achieved that status through America's standards.

For their part, Blacks question the rise of Black male images that are asexual or effeminate, such as Michael Jackson and Prince. While Blacks enjoy seeing the mega-success of any Black person, it's easy to understand the Black male's dilemma when he sees white America embracing these images of maleness. Is this what America wants of Black men? Or, is this what Black men become if they follow the rules of America's game toward becoming a "man."

It is tempting to say that since America's *manhood* is so elusive to Black men, the Black man has created his own definition of manhood. But that would be false. He has not created his own definition of manhood in response to white society. He has created a manhood in response to Black society. A man must be considered a man among his peers, and therefore he must achieve this status through the rules established in the environment around him.

Black men achieve manhood through the use of the rules they have established for *cool*. This is why many a single Black mother tears her hair out when her son is around eleven or twelve. He *has* to be cool; he *wants* to be cool; because he wants to be a man. *Cool* essentially defines *manhood*. Once an adult male is considered cool, his peers consider him a man. America, however, does not consider him a man, because by America's standards he is not a man. If he has not gained certain things that a white man must gain in order to receive this highly coveted title by his peers (which is America itself), then he has not achieved manhood in America's eyes. Of course, it is impossible for him to achieve it, since it requires the cooperation and respect of America itself.

The contradiction between how America perceives cool and how cool really and truly functions is very clear to most Black Americans, but it had been difficult to find any one description that captured America's assumptions about cool until the May 1992 edition of *New York* magazine. In the article "Tough Enough," about rival advertising agencies, we are offered this observation: "FDV often competes with and has been compared with other ad brats, like Goldsmith-Jeffrey & Bond, the bad boys of advertising. Their work is shocking, unsettling, and scandalous—they fall over themselves trying to be cool," says Verdi. "It's attention for attention's sake," adds Follis. The gap between the reality of what cool is and how it functions, and the perception of cool—and how that perception hurts Black men—is an abyss that must be closed.

The white perception of cool is incredibly distorted, very narrow, and therefore damaging. A white male friend of mine, who has discussed the notion with me for years, still perceives cool as simply a style, an arrogance, and he reacts to that image accordingly. It's a testimony to his limited ability to see things differently more than anything else. When people begin studying engineering or higher mathematics they are first taught problem-solving, which is essentially a new way of thinking, a new way of seeing things. Your perceptions of certain words must change. White Americans have such an ingrained perception of the word *cool* that they are unable to see cool as anything other than "rebellious" and "scandalous." Cool to them is an irritation, it's the act of a teenager who is acting out. White America assumes its perception is correct and therefore reacts to it in kind. They vote in tough love, benign neglect, tax cuts, welfare reform, more prisons, more biased college requirements, whatever, all in an attempt to reprimand, train, or control cool. They resent this *child* who they feel won't grow up. That's what they believe cool represents. As Mr. Verdi and Mr. Follis state, it's attention for attention's sake; it's shocking, unsettling, and scandalous. Assuming the owners of the rival ad agency are white, it is safe to say they are *trying* to be cool. But when someone white wants to be cool, which is not *necessary* to becoming a man in his environment, he simply becomes a nuisance.

Black English has afforded Black people many terms that they find are much more expressive and therefore more effective for them than standard English. In some ways, Black English is a classic example of how cool works. So much of what Black people have adopted into their language comes from a stylizing of standard English, and is a reflection of how much standard English, and in turn standard life, is irrelevant.

When I was young we often used the word *ig*. It's a verb. To *ig*. "Oh, wow, man, she *igged* you." I had always assumed it was short for *ignore*, but it's turned out to be more than just a shortcut. When someone *ignored* you, there was a politeness to it; you weren't sure how to interpret it . . . maybe she didn't see you, maybe she was deep in thought, maybe she didn't feel your question required a real response. Maybe a lot of things. But if someone *igged* you, they more than ignored you. You *knew* you had been ignored. You had been deliberately ignored; you had been ignored with an attitude. You were ignored so bad you should be embarrassed. With Black English, the language reflects the manner in which life really happens. *Ignored* is simply not good enough, because it doesn't convey what really happened.

As with the symbols of cool, which we will discuss later, Black English changes rapidly. The language of the streets changes as attitudes change and as actions change. *Ig* is now obsolete. Ig always conveyed an action and an attitude. At one time, to be igged was the worst attitude someone could convey to you without directly speaking to you. It was an insult, a slight. But being igged has lost its weight. There is something more potent and insulting than that. And so the word *ig* has been replaced.

Now the word is *dis*. To dis someone is to disrespect them (or, if you didn't mean it with that much power, to disregard them). Respect is a very important issue right now on the streets. It has always been the main goal of cool, but it has now become a preoccupation among young Blacks; the question being asked of every young Black man who exists on the streets is, How much respect do you deserve and how do you intend to get it? Unfortunately, *respect* and *fear* have become confused.

Therefore to be dissed by someone can be the ultimate insult. And if the person doing the dissing isn't fully prepared, he can get seriously hurt.

The word game of Black English is a very descriptive form of speech, developed out of a need to be more precise about what is going on. Since Black life can be so much more extreme in certain instances, perhaps there needs to be a stronger word to describe it.

Cool is another descriptive word. It most likely originated during the jazz era. The frantic, pulsating, sporadic rhythms of jazz, which expressed the restlessness and rebelliousness of the musicians, were wild and hot. Eventually the musicians would calm it down, "play it *cool*."

Cool was soon adopted as a description of a man with harnessed emotions, controlled aggression, and angry discontent. He conveyed a contradiction of attitudes; while he walked cool and handled himself calmly and confidently, there was no mistaking that inside he was hot, angry, and able to cause great harm if necessary. Cool became the term to describe an image of harnessed power, combined with style and confidence.

This contradiction in attitude is the very reason why cool is so difficult to achieve, but it is this very contradiction that is essential to life in the streets.

Jazz provided more than just the word *cool*. Jazz and the men who performed it were the personification of cool. Jazz gave voice to the clash of personalities and experiences in the cities of America.

Because of the sheer artistry of jazz, America had to take notice. Jazz created a whole new aesthetic, and described for white America the rhythms and different styles and experiences of Black America.

America gained respect for an emerging Black culture which had created an art form white America could neither ignore nor duplicate. Most important, this art form evolved on its own, with no preoccupation with America's music or America's acceptance. This afforded jazz and its jazzmen a level of respect that Black Americans (and particularly Black men) had never received before. Black culture had presented America with countless forms of self-expression—musical, culinary, rhetorical, literary, spiritual, communal, and on and on. America had stolen from its Black culture for centuries, as Blacks were well aware all along; now they were getting their due.

Jazz evolved from ragtime and blues into a cultural phenomenon. By the 1950s jazz was creating its own offspring. When Miles Davis came along, jazz found its media darling. He spoke the language and had the look that white America felt comfortable with (as the "Miles Davis wore khakis" Gap ads today remind us). But Miles Davis, who had enjoyed a privileged childhood, demonstrated the arrogance afforded a child of privilege. However, his arrogance was uniquely Black. In some ways, he and his fellow musicians such as Dizzy Gillespie, John Coltrane, and Charlie Parker defined the attitude of cool. Frankly, to many Blacks, these earlier musicians were really the personification of a Black male manhood—a style, an aesthetic. Miles Davis simply became America's acceptable example of Black male manhood, a palatable personality for the media to embrace.

Jazz musicians may also be responsible for setting the tone for drugs and alcohol as an expression of Black manhood. While these musicians resorted to drugs and alcohol for artistic survival—because as creative people, life had to be free and crazy for them—getting high translated to a style, a symbol, of being cool.

If a jazz piece is heard as though it were a conversation between its performers, then Miles Davis always hosted the gathering. He was the urbane host who found the right subject, presented it, and then let everyone else talk. He would then intervene when things got hot or when the conversation started to wind down. He might put things back in perspective or shake it all up by throwing some shit in the pot or changing the subject. Then he'd step back again, serving interesting conversational hors d'oeuvres while his guests enjoyed their repartee. Very few white Americans were invited to the party, and Miles found no reason for them to be there. If they came it was as paying customers; his guests, the performers, were the party. These other people were there to pay the rent; they were not allowed to really participate. When he performed in concert, Miles conveyed the fact that he was not some hired help performing with a tin can on the ground. You were lucky he let you pay to come to his house.

This attitude personified the growing pride Black men were gaining in their unique style and attitude within this society. By the early seventies Miles would show up late; he would perform with his back turned to the audience; he would not deign to banter or entertain the audience. His loyalties were to his fellow musicians; his respect was for them, and in turn the only respect he wanted was *from* them. Tap dancing for white folks to earn their respect or money was never on the agenda. And yet they came, because the music and even the message was profound.

This is not to give Miles all the credit, but only to use his style as a personification of cool. This same attitude is found in other performers, of course. A good example is Gregory Hines. A friend and I watched a PBS special together on tap dancing. My friend, a Black man, commented that he didn't understand why Hines got all the praise he did when other dancers featured on the show seemed so much more precise, cleaner, more acrobatic. To me the answer was clear: "It's political." Hines dances like jazz. He improvises, he syncopates, he dances with attitude, he stops and starts, he slides briefly without becoming the eighth wonder of the world, and then he stops to let one toe express itself. If you don't get it, too bad; if you do, you might be invited to the next show. Others dance to dazzle—actually they "perform"; and to some Blacks it's "for the money."

Not to overdo this point, but I have also felt that comedians like Richard Pryor and, as a result of him, Eddie Murphy were an evolution in Black maleness. No longer playing for acceptance by whites, comedians are writing jokes in the vernacular of their community. The complaint that Murphy "relies" on vulgarity and swearing as an easy way to get laughs totally ignores his brilliance as a comedian. Murphy has struggled with staying completely loyal to his community. (Loyalty, as described later in the book, is essential to remaining cool.) He conceives his humor from whence he came. When Eddie first appeared on TV, my friends and I marveled at how familiar he seemed; every junior high school class had a guy like Eddie Murphy in it—funny, daring, and dangerous. (He's dangerous because that quick wit can entertain you one minute and stab you in the heart the next, depending on how you act.) If he didn't curse, he wouldn't sound real to his audience. You can join his audience if you like; if you don't, that's not his problem.

When Eddie Murphy imitated James Brown, and even Buckwheat, by singing imperceptible words, Black people were hysterical. Eddie knew that we had all grown up trying to understand what James was saying. The humor was for those who really knew James Brown. If you weren't hip to James, you might not get the joke. Too bad.

By the way, it's really interesting what happens when Black men tend to their own business and are loyal to their own audience. An example recently emerged for me. I was talking with a twenty-five-year-old white male acquaintance about his dating life. We segued into the recognition that when women sleep around they are considered sluts but when men do it they are studs. To illustrate a point about women and their sexuality and a woman's search for the all-around man who can make her happy sexually, intellectually, spiritually, with humor and sometimes valor, I asked him if he'd seen Spike Lee's *She's Gotta Have It*.

"No, Spike Lee is mean to whites in his films," he answered. I was stunned. I had to go back through the films I'd seen. "Spike Lee isn't mean to whites in his films," I protested. "He's simply not concerned with whites in his films." But it fell on deaf ears. I, in my simplistic way, concluded that if Blacks don't address whites in everything they do, the word gets around, and therefore the perception is spread that that Black person is hostile. But many Blacks, in their craft, are simply indifferent to whites.

Street Life

We have to begin our look at cool on the streets of this country, because that is where this desperate need for a code of manhood originated. Street cool is the stage of cool that is angry, daring, and impulsive. It is also the mode of cool that deals the most in style and symbols. Life on the streets is fast-paced and dangerous; it is survival against the gravest odds. This kind of survival is not what you find in a controlled environment, not the same thing football is to a young boy in the suburbs. It's real survival; it's your life you're playing with. There is little time for any discourse or subtle exchange of thought that would put your cool across. Your cool must be conveyed first through your appearance, next through your attitude, and finally through your ability to defend yourself. All of these elements come together to help you survive and conquer the dangers and obstacles on the streets.

These streets are angry, violent, dangerous, complicated, unpredictable, and relentless. But, believe it or not, the streets are also fun, familiar, filled with adventure, family, friends, and energy. These streets are the playground to millions of young Black children.

Childhood, no matter where you come from, is always the same. It is filled with challenge, curiosity, and growth. Most average Americans are able to experience this growth in their own backyard, or on the football field at their school, or on family excursions. Many underprivileged Black children experience this in their neighborhood—in trash-filled parks, deserted playgrounds, empty lots, dark hallways, subway stations, etc. When a young boy in suburbia challenges himself by finally winning a spot on the football team, a young city kid might have to challenge himself by telling a frightening and potentially dangerous boy to kiss his behind.

Cool began in the streets of urban America. It emerged from a desperate need for guidelines concerning maturity that incorporated the strange challenges of street life, of life without the tools of traditional American manhood, and of a life where life itself is the only thing you possess that's of any value. In a country where manhood is determined by the levels of risk you're willing to take—and where usually that risk is demonstrated through money, America's most valued entity—the young

Black boy must demonstrate that risk with his life, since it is often, unfortunately, the only valued entity *he* possesses.

Manhood is something determined between males. While it is certainly about a man's relationship with women as well, it is first determined by other males.

In most instances a young boy is taught to be a man by the men around him, usually beginning with his father. But cool is a cycle. By now, many adult Black men are third- or fourth-generation inner city men. This will mean that they too have been raised with the rules of cool as their definition of manhood. Therefore cool can get passed on by the father, as the rules of manhood and maturity get passed on by a father figure in the larger society. And what it means to be cool, to be a man, will be defined by that father's values. A father in the inner city may have a balanced view, steering his son cautiously through being cool while also teaching him to become a man in a more traditional way; but this is a difficult and often impossible task as the inner city gets more and more brutal and as being cool becomes more and more of a mandate. If the father is absent, or if he is a teenager and/or immature (by America's standards) himself, these boys will eventually learn to be "men" in the streets, where "being cool" is the defining factor. Or, they may try to get their image of manhood from the media's image of a man. (It may be equally hard for white boys to live up to media images of manhood.)

The media's image of manhood is a decidedly wrong one for a young Black boy growing up in the streets to follow, because not only does the boy not have the tools to achieve this image (those tools usually being money and a support system called *America*), but he has no real understanding of how that man standing on the screen evolved from the little boy he once was. The circumstances that brought that little boy to become that man on the screen have little to do with the road this young Black boy must travel.

That boy's journey will be a very bumpy one, filled with obstacles. These obstacles will not simply cause setbacks, as they do in the average American life, they can cause serious harm; a young Black boy can lose not only his potential for, or dreams of, success—he can lose his life. Life on the streets is no picnic, and no joke.

A young boy is only human. He can't spend every waking moment defending himself, proving himself, being challenged and overcoming those challenges. If he does, he will soon be exhausted, weakened, vulnerable. So, he must learn to protect himself.

In a chaotic existence, protection is both physical and mental. You must protect your personal safety and your sanity. Learning what protects is one's process toward manhood; when one is finally deemed cool, he has successfully learned to protect himself and is able to convey to others, without words, that he can. Conveying his physical and mental strength is essential to being able to live a relatively calm existence in the streets— he won't be challenged often and he won't be picked on; instead he'll be respected and looked up to by others (who will want to learn what he knows). He will have achieved the label of *cool*. And he will be considered a man by other men in his environment.

Unfortunately, protection and respect have become almost impossible to achieve on the streets of America. The streets become increasingly brutal as life in America becomes increasingly merciless. When I was growing up, a boy surviving a fight with sticks and rocks, perhaps even knives, might earn respect from his peers. Today on those same streets, respect is gained through guns and money. Real guns, big money.

In the movie *Grand Canyon* Danny Glover talks with a group of Black teenage boys who are about to do harm to Kevin Kline. He asks the boys who is in charge, and one boy identifies himself, shows Glover his gun, and steps over for a private talk. Glover asks the boy/man to let him do his job and tow the man's car. Finally, the boy/man agrees. He then asks Glover, "If I didn't have this gun, would you ask my permission?" Glover responds honestly, "If you didn't have that gun, we wouldn't be talking." The boy/man walks away and says, "You see? No gun, no respect." While the possibility of a conversation like this ever taking place is the fantasy of Hollywood, it did capture an important reality: Respect and fear are synonymous. It also shows something more important: This young man thinks he deserves Glover's respect. But does he? Respect for what? He is still a child. Respect is something earned over time; it should not be expected from a grown man by a young man simply because he has reached a certain age. But respect and maturity are lost on the streets, where life is getting cheaper and cheaper and respect is getting more and more expensive.

The Symbols of Cool
(or, What Is Hip?)

At about age twelve a young girl begins to menstruate, and the realities of being female become a part of her life. Thus, through physical forces, a female child becomes a woman. She has to take responsibility for her body, and for herself as a woman, at a very young age. She is relatively well prepared for this occurrence: Her mother has been menstruating for years and tampons or sanitary napkins are present in the home; health education class explains to her what is happening in her body; and her friends or older sisters have experienced it. Therefore a young girl becomes very aware of herself as she matures. For many young girls, their first period is an occasion for their mothers to have a brief discussion with them. As Clair Huxtable once explained to twelve-year-old Rudy on *The Cosby Show*, "You are a woman now." "No I'm not," Rudy protested. "I'm only twelve." Her mother smiled knowingly and said that nonetheless, she is now a young woman, and is now able to bring beautiful children into this world.

At thirteen, young Jewish boys are given a bar mitzvah, introducing them to manhood. The idea is usually just as foreign to them as being a woman was to Rudy, but they have been expecting this ritual of maturity all year, and have been coached and prepped for quite some time before the ceremony. And while they might leave the ceremony and go play Nintendo, the concept of manhood has been introduced into their consciousness.

In the same way that nature introduces womanhood to a young girl, manhood must be introduced into a young boy's consciousness. Yes, a young boy goes through puberty and his body is also changing, but puberty's relationship to manhood and the responsibilities he now has as a man are not conveyed to him through nature. Perhaps it is only because young girls begin to menstruate that societies feel boys must acknowledge their budding reality as men.

In a life where there are no rituals, no rites of passage, and few fathers in the homes to explain the concepts of manhood, young boys attempt to define it for themselves. Their definitions of manhood become shaped not by the realities of puberty or by the rules of the larger society, but by the images and symbols that depict manhood in their environment. Young boys' definition of manhood are being shaped more and more by the depiction of manhood they see on movie screens. And the movie screens are more and more sensationalizing a manhood that is perhaps *part* of the boy's reality but is not the *total* of his reality. *Grand Canyon* and *Parenthood* don't get shown in Harlem, but *Under Siege, Juice,* and *New Jack City* do.

Symbols of manhood are really imitations of manhood more than they are honest symbols of growth and maturity. If an older and tougher boy, who has gained the respect/fear of many, is wearing a leather jacket with an eight-ball emblazoned on the back, that becomes the hippest thing to wear and becomes symbolic of being cool.

Hip and *cool* are not synonymous. Those outside of the Black community often confuse these two terms and think they are descriptions of the same thing. Hip simply refers to being in, the latest, "bad," while cool is an attitude, a lifestyle, an achievement.

And both terms are becoming archaic; Black English changes over time, so that the language remains fresh and exclusive. *Cool* has been used and misused so often, and the concept of cool has been imitated so much, that the word is almost obsolete. But its significance has not changed, at least not in street life.

■　　■　　■

Symbols are tangible—they signify something and are attainable. The elements that make a boy a man in this country are not only intangible, they're subtle and difficult to understand or attain. But clothes, haircuts, and jewelry are real, and are representative of cunning and strength; in order to have these things it's assumed you have these qualities.

However, symbols often have very little to do with manhood. The symbols of cool and manhood have more to do with conveying an understanding of style or your ability to defend yourself than with maturity. Real cool always manages to convey an unwillingness to follow trends—thus the coolest boy is the one who doesn't *follow* the trend but *sets* it.

The rebelliousness inherent in the symbols of cool is obviously a catch-22. Cool says if you follow society's sense of style you're not cool, you're a follower. But America says if you don't follow society's sense of style you're not likely to succeed in this society, and that if you do it will be as an outlaw or an outsider, usually a very difficult journey toward success. (Of course, another catch-22 is that America rewards those who do manage to make it through the outsider route. America's philosophy of "freedom" has to do with choices, allowing individuals to choose their own lifestyle. While the lifestyle of an outsider may be arduous, it is possible to succeed in that lifestyle. But *outsider* and *outlaw* are also not necessarily synonymous.)

A man's ability to defend himself is at the very core of cool. It must be understood immediately in the streets, otherwise he will spend his every waking moment proving this ability. Conveying this ability becomes a combination of appearance and attitude; thus the symbols of cool, which change from year to year, and from town to town. These trappings must convey that you are *down*, you know what's happening, you are *one of us*, you ain't *soft*. If you are soft—unable to fight and win, if necessary, or, even worse, afraid to fight and win, and it's obvious—there's a place for you, but it isn't on the streets.

Thirteen is a tender age for a boy to make life choices, but in the streets it is the most crucial time in his development.

Paul is an average-looking kid who lives in my apartment building on New York's upper Riverside Drive area. His mother has a good mid-level job at a major corporation, with responsibilities and good pay. I've never met Paul's father. When Paul was about thirteen or fourteen years old I noticed he had a crowd of boys with him all the time. Although Paul was soft-spoken, he was tall and confident. The boys seemed to follow him, and it became apparent that he was a leader in the group. Occasionally another boy would have center stage, but it was always time to go when Paul felt it was time to go. He wasn't a dictator—he checked with one or two of the others for agreement—but he did seem to command a bit more respect than anyone else in the group. Paul wasn't living in a rough part of Harlem, but he went to a tough junior high school and managed to survive it without landing in jail, punking out, dropping out, or being alienated. Therefore he seemed a reasonable candidate to talk about cool.

It turned out Paul was an MC at parties. This is the guy who plays the records and ultimately makes or breaks the party. A good MC dictates the success of a party.

I asked Paul if he was considered cool. He hemmed and hawed and talked about being an MC at parties. I pressed again, "Are you considered cool?" Finally, he said, "I guess so."

Apparently cool is not something you decide for yourself. If you state that you're cool, you immediately aren't. Cool people are rarely challenged, because it is understood that they can protect themselves. But if you declare that you are cool, usually through wearing certain clothes or acting a certain way, you'll get challenged right away. *Oh, you think you're cool? We'll see how cool you are.*

"Are you cool because you run the music at the parties?"

"Yeah. And because me and my friends wear nice clothes. We don't go out there with old sneakers and stuff."

"So, is that what cool is? Is it your clothes?"

"Yeah."

"So, anybody wearing the right clothes can be considered cool?"

"Nah. It's not that simple. There are a lot of guys who wear stuff just to look cool, but they're not."

"How do you know they're not."

" 'Cause they just come to school dressed in stuff and they don't have anything behind it. You can tell they're soft."

"How can you tell?"

"Because they try too hard. They just stand there, imitating other guys, but you can tell they're scared."

"What are they afraid of?"

"They're afraid of someone approaching them. They might have to fight or something."

"But why would you approach them? Why would they have to fight?"

"Well, they're really asking for trouble by the way they dress and by their attitude. They really think they're cool but you know they aren't, so you challenge them. It's too bad, but that's the way it is. Maybe it's not so bad, because it teaches some of them a lesson."

And so, a young boy gets taught he's not cool. He wore the symbols of cool but didn't have anything behind it.

Maybe one day a boy will be able to dress any way he likes, but for now in the streets your style becomes a symbol of your knowledge of those streets and of your ability to protect yourself. Those who have not "earned" their cool are easily recognized. If they're wearing the symbols, they're demonstrating "imitation cool" and they stand out a mile away. This is one reason why traditionally the styles on the streets change so quickly. The uncool quickly adopt the cool style. When this happens, it is time for what's considered cool to change.

Clothes are the beginning of the symbols of cool. A boy doesn't learn the correct way to dress by looking in magazines. In the inner city, your style of dress conveys a great deal about you—your boldness, your awareness of what's "the latest," the amount of money you or your parents have to spend, your worth, your self-esteem, your mettle, your cool. We've all read in the newspapers about young boys being killed for a leather jacket. As we shake our heads in disgust at how cheap life is on the streets, we're missing something that is integral to cool: You can't wear an expensive leather jacket unless you have the mettle to wear it. You must prove first to yourself, and then to others, that you can wear something so expensive *and* keep it. You're conveying to others, whether intentional or not, that you think you have the stuff to wear something; but if you don't, as Paul explains, you can get yourself hurt.

Manhood and cool reflect an internal growth. Symbols are

external and reflect only a boy's understanding of how manhood *looks*.

How Does Street Cool Look?

A young Black boy will quickly learn that some of the older boys he sees are cool and some are not. He might then adopt the cool ones' style so that he too can seem older, stronger, hipper. The boys who are cool don't get picked on as much, they don't get challenged as much, so maybe if he looks cool, he will avoid the hassles.

But cool cannot be bought in the stores. Symbols of cool can be bought, but cool cannot. And so, as with the boy in Paul's school, he invites trouble. He gets picked on even more.

Cool is a combination of elements. Certainly your appearance establishes your level of cool, but that is not how cool looks. Cool is an attitude, and that attitude is self-confidence.

The attitude is a manifestation of your basic personality coupled with the confidence you gain in knowing you can handle yourself. Handling yourself on the streets can mean a lot of things—physical confrontations, brushes with the law, manipulation of authority figures, finesse with the ladies, etc. Through experiences, experimentation, and risk-taking, a young man learns that he can handle himself. He becomes streetwise, in tune with his mental and physical capabilities. By dodging cars, getting in street fights, going after the finest girls, testing drugs, conning the police, jumping roofs, a street kid learns his abilities within his limited resources. He doesn't have the same tools for testing himself that more privileged Americans have, so his environment demands different skills. Those skills will be valuable to him, as long as he remains in his environment.

He can't succumb to the limits of his environments, though; the rules of cool won't let him. To survive on the streets you must be considered cool. To be considered cool, you must strive for self-confidence, and once it is achieved you must exude it.

Survival does not mean jail, it does not mean becoming a junkie, it does not mean welfare. Surviving does not mean stagnation or complacency, or accepting a certain situation. A boy cannot buy the best sneakers at age sixteen and still be wearing them at thirty-five and be considered cool by his peers.

Unfortunately, cool is determined by others. It is not something a boy can deem himself. Cool is also not something that a boy achieves alone. He can wake up every morning and declare himself cool until he's blue in the face, but that won't make him cool. He has to be anointed "cool" by his peers. He must first be considered cool by his peers to feel its benefits. Once anointed, he enjoys the ultimate in self-esteem, something in short supply in the neighborhoods of poverty.

Cool provides protection—He's cool, don't mess with him. And it provides self-esteem because he is looked up to and respected. A boy's ability to defend himself is at the core of cool in the streets. It must be understood that he is able to handle himself, otherwise he will spend every waking moment trying to prove this ability. But as he tries to prove it, through fighting and arguing and standing up for himself in situations, he proves it to himself. The angrier he gets and less fearful he feels, the more his attitude will change. He will one day find himself considered cool by his friends.

Rap artists today reflect all these elements. They've all got the look, the attitude, and their ability to defend themselves is demonstrated in their videos. They wave guns and talk tough to constantly demonstrate that they're not soft. (Teenagers now comment on how soft the members of Run-DMC appear, a dangerous thing for a rap group.) One problem for rappers that's being played out on the news every day is how to *stay* cool. Success has a way of taking away that anger, that edge, and ultimately that ability to defend yourself. When you make your livelihood based on your aggression, anger, toughness, etc., big money can soften some or all of that. Kris Kross, a duo of young boys who are slowly growing up, is a good example. They never smile, they never seem happy. While they sing about "Sprite," which is probably making them a lot of money, they almost grimace. That's because heaven forbid their fellow homeboys should detect that they are having a good time on the other side.

So, Who Is Cool in the Streets?

It would be fun to write that Denzel Washington is cool, Laurence Fishburne is cool, Keenan Ivory Wayans is cool, and so on. It would be fun to set myself up as the arbiter of cool. But nope, it's not that easy. Everyone has his or her own images of cool, and I wouldn't think of defining it here.

I can tell you this, though: It is cool to survive, especially when we're talking about the life-and-death existence of the streets.

Escape from the streets is very cool, depending on how it's achieved.

Attitude may be the most important element of cool. You can't buy attitude. It comes from self-confidence in successfully handling yourself within your environment.

When a boy begins to define his manhood by the rules of the streets, his entire outlook on life may soon be completely different from what society would like it to be. The streets are filled with so much anger and deprivation that society as a whole gets blamed. Therefore, depending on which group he's involved with, the rules of the streets can be anti-society, anti-rules, or anti-authority.

This lifestyle is the most potentially dangerous element to the rules of the streets. A young boy who is caught in the streets of America will begin to understand and accept the fact that the people he must please and prove himself to are often the most negative influences in our society. He then loses all desire and potential to conform to or participate in what this society dictates to him. (It took me a minute to decide if *dictates* is the right word. Members of the mainstream would argue that *provides* for him would be more accurate and appropriate. Unfortunately, that is our view, not his. The very point I'm trying to make is that at this point he is following the rules of a cool that has rejected the larger society, and which feels that if a boy adheres to that society's rules he is a punk, to be picked on and ridiculed, and forced to change. If he cannot, he had better move away from the neighborhood.)

If a young boy sees no escape or alternative to street life, he must learn to become a man of the streets; his manhood and maturity get defined in those terms and he will see himself as soft, a faggot, a pussy, if he does not adhere to those terms.

The boy who is caught in this spiral will have a very interesting relationship with the police. When there is no father present or if his father also adheres to the negative side of cool, the police might serve as a father figure, offering limits (the positive possibility) or something to rebel against (the negative possibility). The police might also represent *the white man* (regardless of the officer's color or gender).

The boy who is forced by his environment to live with poverty, fear, and violence becomes angry. That anger can potentially destroy him. So his friends, and maybe his father, teach him to be cool. Playing the Dozens (also known as sounding or snapping) is one way young boys teach each other to harness their anger. *Yo' mama liked it.* This statement implies that one boy had sex with the other boy's mother. A very degrading notion, yes? Actually, these two boys might be in a playful argument, or they might be in a playful argument that's about to get very serious. The Dozens is not a game, it's a method of teaching each other how to deal with anger—when to lose your cool and "throw down" (fight), and when to laugh it off. I don't think anyone made up The Dozens thinking, "We need something to teach young Black boys how to deal with their anger." No, it just happened. The Dozens functions; it isn't just an example of how little Black people respect each other, as some people are quick to assume.

This mechanism of cool is as basic as the cool developed during the captive experience. Once again, it is all about physical and emotional survival. Fear and anger are emotions to be conquered. A boy must learn to harness anger without destroying it. Cool becomes a demonstration of his ability to convey the power behind that anger, in subtle but definite ways. Cool is the confidence he earns when he has mastered these abilities.

The boy learns to use his anger to make himself stronger and, he hopes, invincible. With this invincibility he may become *cold*. He knows how to protect himself, he tests his strength and stamina with drugs or alcohol, he looks for the finest women to have on his arm, he wins battles or uses street cunning to escape certain situations.

He is usually terrified of letting his girlfriend (or anyone else) see how human he is. Unfortunately, in most cases in the inner city she is just as afraid to actually see him as a frail and frightened human being (which is what cool is designed to hide). So, the tragedy is that when he inches his way toward being real, she panics and betrays his trust.

When the young kid growing up in the separate world of America's streets pursues and wins a fine-looking girl, he feels proud of himself. But when he realizes or understands that there is a whole society—supposedly the one he lives in—that doesn't recognize her beauty, he is frustrated, angry, confused, and insulted. If all men can't see her beauty, then to him she is not beautiful. And since America has yet to acknowledge the Black woman's beauty, many young men experience this turmoil. If he learns to discount America's ignorance of her beauty (in other words, if he keeps his mind in the confines of his environment), he won't care what America thinks and he will care all the more what his peer group thinks. And *they* think she's *fine*.

As a Black woman, I have a problem with this also. I talked with young women for this book and mentioned that when a boy chases a girl, she feels "pretty." These girls laughed at my use of that word. While they were saying I was using this dumb, archaic word, I couldn't help but feel that Black girls are not used to being referred to as "pretty," and therefore have come to find the word itself silly. Also, when I've talked to young white males about America's rejection of the Black female's good looks, they have remarked that that is changing. After all, they say, there are lots of television shows and movies showing attractive Black women. Yes, but those shows are designed for Black audiences. Black female attractiveness must be recognized and appreciated by all American men, just as white images are.

Many street kids are duped into thinking that doing or dealing drugs is cool. In the hard-core inner city, where the perception is that there is little chance of real escape, the drug culture has a lot to offer. The drug culture presents all kinds of avenues for demonstrating manhood and mettle. If a boy is proving himself to a peer group that found its manhood in the drug culture, he will embrace it as well. It certainly offers the illusion and the trappings of cool—money, women, and perceived power. Unfortunately, it begins to unravel. The drug culture forces young men to go deeper and deeper into a dead-end situation. Boys who never let go of the need to be cool, and who are trying to prove it in the wrong crowd, become more entrenched in that world, and eventually end up in jail, addicted, or dead. To those who know nothing else, jail becomes another world to conquer, at that point, unfortunately, because their lives depend on showing how strong and invincible they are. Their new peer group is way beyond the silly games a boy indulges in while trying to prove his manhood in the streets.

The danger of cool is that it is dictated by your peer group. Young men must be careful of the friends they choose when they're growing up. Unfortunately, there are few he can really trust on the streets of America; and even those who are trustworthy may not have any answers about how to escape cool's negative drawbacks.

The spiral of cool can go crashing downward for those who are caught in an environment or peer group that constantly forces them to prove their cool through increasingly negative behavior.

Working at McDonald's, or someplace comparable, is not considered cool, because you'll never make any *real* money. So a young man may get caught up in crime, at first to be cool but eventually to continue making any kind of money. Jail is then inevitable. Alas, the problem of jobs in the inner cities is a bigger one than this book can address. Without intervention from the larger society to provide real and abundant jobs in these neighborhoods, many of the problems these young men face, that make cool their only means of achieving self-esteem and manhood, will always exist. Right now they are faced with the option of wearing ridiculous uniforms and serving hamburgers (or delivering groceries, or moving stock) while making minimum wage. This is not cool and it will ensure that respect from peers will be a long time in coming.

As Elaine Jones of the National Association for the Advancement of Colored People (NAACP) so passionately explained during an interview on Black Entertainment Network, her father and many Black men of his generation (including my grandfather) worked as Pullman porters. That job allowed her father to provide for a wife and five children. Her mother also worked, as a teacher. Her father earned his respect the American way, something today's young men are not given a chance to do. It has also been documented time and again that when a young man is given a chance to really work, his co-workers become his family, with the potential to replace the gang in that role. Jobs would have to be provided en masse to make a real difference in communities stricken with poverty, because it simply isn't cool to work in McDonald's.

Lawlessness or prison can become an inevitable part of life in today's inner city. Some housing projects in this country have special express buses that go directly to the prisons. The message is there for those who get caught up in the negative side of cool's pull.

Jail and drugs are not cool in and of themselves; universally, though, cool is survival. Jail and drugs are not survival to most of the young Black boys and girls in this country, but they are often so much a part of their environment that they must use them to prove their mettle to each other, and to challenge themselves.

Mom and Dad and the Church
(or, Who's in Charge?)

The lack of a "mature male" (by America's definition) is a pervasive problem in the life of a young boy growing up in the world of street cool. Unfortunately, many adult males who are present in this environment are still following the dictates of cool themselves, still seeking that level of cool that will free them and make them feel as though they are men, to be re-spected and looked up to.

In homes without a father, the mother tries to substitute. Maturity is organic. It doesn't just happen, and contrary to what cool is set up to do, young boys cannot teach themselves to be men. A young girl might enjoy the title "woman" by virtue of her menstrual cycle, but teenage mothers are rarely full-fledged, mature women. Another unfortunate result of the lack of a mature man in the home is that *she* might never become a mature woman. *Maturity is organic.* A mature woman makes a mature man and a mature man makes a mature woman.

What is most sad in a home where a man or woman is not mature or has not reached a higher level of emotional growth is that as the children grow and begin to challenge their parents, the parents respond with force rather than reason. If Dad is in the home and has yet to mature, his son will soon become a threat to him. As he begins to feel his control slipping, he will challenge his son instead of grooming him. This situation is certainly not a Black phenomenon, but cool is, and that is what the son will turn to for direction.

In a chaotic home, or when life itself is full of danger, vices, confusion, fear, frustration, whatever, a woman who is alone and who faces struggles as life moves on may turn to the church for answers. But, alas, it is seldom an answer for her son.

Religion and cool don't mix well, because religion is contrary to the life of cool. All the things that being cool in the streets demands are sins in the church. Religion is also perceived as the last beacon of hope for the defeated, and defeat is a state that is inherently uncool. Religion dictates that you are not invincible, and it teaches that you should believe in something that is stronger than yourself to guide you. Anyone in the streets knows that no one is coming down from the heavens to protect you. Santa Claus won't climb in your window on Christmas Eve, and God won't be there when you're in a fight. The subtle possibility that God can be a way of life, an inner guide, is lost when violence and poverty are a daily occurrence.

Still, many embrace religion in the inner city with such totality that they become zombies in the eyes of others—selling the *Watchtower* on the corner, speaking in tongues, believing in the Lord more than anything else, loving the church more than their children (or so it sometimes seems to the child). Therefore, young boys reject religion out of hand. If a mother forces it, her authority begins to lose its potency; once her son says no to her about one thing, a pattern has been set.

The single mother in the life of the streets must learn to follow her son's cool and not fight against it. She must prune and protect. She must above all understand, or she will lose all control. When she loses control she will be blamed, by the wayward father and by society, for having failed to make her son a good man—something that is nearly impossible for her to do alone.

Cool has many meanings and purposes. For those who need it, cool is a mechanism for survival, a symbol of strength and prowess, and from that strength it becomes a vehicle for self-esteem. When a person is truly cool there exists for him an unspoken respect throughout the community, and from this respect comes a sense of self-worth.

In the streets, being cool might be the only way to be left in peace in a place where peace is in short supply.

So, this is cool in the streets of America. Cool is a system for many young Black men, but not all. Since most Black people have experienced the inner city at some generational stage, cool has touched all our lives, and all Black Americans are keenly aware of its existence—not as some interesting little cultural phenomenon, but as a powerfully important, and often disturbing, reality.

Street cool is one level, one mode. It has evolved and changed and grown as Black Americans have grown. But its dictates—for better or worse, as we will see in future chapters—still influence our daily lives, no matter who we are, where we go, or what we do.

chapter two

Revolutionary Cool

"I don't want nobody

to give me nuthin'.

(Open up the door,

and I'll get it myself.)"

—James Brown

eginning in the late fifties and continuing through the early seventies, the Black community of America was in the throes of a struggle for liberation. After having been "freed" from captivity in 1865, "liberation" was just beginning to take place for Black Americans a hundred years later.

The revolution began in the 1950s with the civil rights movement, which had been shaped and defined by the southern, and more traditional, Black American, and was masterminded and nurtured in the Black churches. With the help of television, the struggle of Black America was given a face and a voice. Many leaders and spokespersons emerged at this time, all reflecting different voices, different styles and symbols, and different political and emotional viewpoints. Stokely Carmichael (Kwame Ture) and Angela Davis spoke to Black Ivy Leaguers; West Coast leaders such as the Black Panther Party's Huey Newton, H. Rap Brown and Eldridge Cleaver captured young Black males; the East Coast and urban cities experienced the Nation of Islam and Malcolm X; and there was the Southern Christian Leadership Conference (SCLC) and the Student Nonviolent Coordinating Committee (SNCC) in the South and on college campuses. While some people were reading *The Autobiography Of Malcolm X*, others were buying *Muhammad Speaks* on street corners, and still others attended protest marches against the war in Vietnam. Some people smoked marijuana for enlightenment, while others read the Koran or the Red Book for the same reason.

While all these different voices and stimuli were in the air, the binding thread for everyone was *enlightenment*. Being informed, aware, smart, worldly, and educated (about yourself as a Black person in this world) was the order of business. This process created a sort of permanent awareness in the minds of Black Americans.

I watched a talk show recently which featured an ignorant, somewhat toothless, stringy-haired white man who announced, "There isn't one nigger smarter than me in this whole world" (or something very similar). A Black man in the audience stood up to the microphone, laughed a bit, and then pointed out—without anger, without rage, without even intensity—that the bigoted white man was simply trying to make him feel bad about himself. And that that wasn't ever going to happen. Instead he felt sorry for the white man (remember *To Kill a Mockingbird*?), because no matter what the bigot said he could never make this Black man feel bad about himself. Those days, he proudly stated, were over.

We all have the fifties, sixties, and early seventies for this wonderful and irreversible reality. This gentleman in the audience was a Black man of the nineties. The eighties tried very hard to reverse this pride, and tragically it did succeed, but only with America's very young Black children. The racist eighties were unsuccessful with the children of the revolution, who were the main target.

Cool was beginning to reach a plateau. The only cool that had existed before the revolutionary sixties was street cool, which was designed to help a boy survive life in the ghetto. By the sixties, street cool had succeeded in doing that.

I'm sure you have noticed that America's language changes to accommodate its growing awareness of changes in Black America and in the country itself. We have gone from *ghetto* to *inner city*, and I'm not sure why. In this book I am certainly talking about communities where Black people live in concentrated numbers, but I am mostly talking about the hundreds of thousands of boys who live and thrive in the streets. They can be found in integrated communities, and in middle-class families, but most are found in the heart of the Black community within a family that lacks resources, and are educated in schools that neither care about them nor stimulate them mentally.

While *ghetto* became *inner city*, *colored* and *Negro* became *Black*, and recently—amid much debate and resistance from some—*Black* has become *African American*. Usually the community can sense the change coming, but the recent change to *African American* came out of nowhere for me, and I have not adopted it. While the term acknowledges that Black people are Americans, it sounds too much like we are immigrants, for my taste.

Many young Black men of the streets had achieved the definitions of street cool. Among their peers, they were cool; they had reached their definition of manhood. But soon they were busting at the seams. Why conquer the streets only to have to live there? It was time to broaden the spectrum, to grow up and out.

If you trace cool—its origins and its function—you will be able to see an entire group of people mature as a race. That is not to imply that Black Americans are individually immature, but Black Americans have been racially, economically, and politically immature. The sixties as a time of "growing up and out" is a very real notion. The world was changing for Black Americans. Cool was there to guide Black males as they broke out of their physical and mental space.

Cool is ultimately about survival. When a man reaches the limits of his environment he has to grow or die; his mind must have a place to grow. He might physically remain in the ghetto, but if he is mentally impoverished, he will explode. Freedom is choice, and when you have enough intellect and information to make other choices, you might choose to stay. If you have chosen to stay, you feel less oppressed, less enslaved, less of a captive—because you know you can leave.

When society presents few choices, cool responds with many negative avenues for a boy's growth. At one time, there was a dangerous threat that cool would create a world of madness and mayhem for a young boy to grow into, (and that is true again today, another era in which American society offers no avenues for growth).

However, the revolution offered many new, and very positive, choices. Enslavement is in the mind. And so is liberation . . .

The sixties became a time of self-discovery and self-awareness. Black people began to learn and appreciate their history. They were conquering their fears—fears of their own past, fears of the outer society, fears that had been falsely instilled in them in order to enslave them. Since the truth was not readily available in the schools, self-education became the order of business. For the first time, "learning" became very cool, and, also for the first time, the lessons were refreshingly positive. But these were different lessons than those found in schools.

Again, one of the unfortunate realities of life in the streets of America is that often the only thing you possess of any value is your life. So street cool dictated that a young man prove himself—prove his worth, his fearlessness, his manhood, his cool—by using his very life. The revolution, though, taught Black Americans, and young Black men in particular, about "nation building," and about "genocide." Suddenly, a young man had something more valuable than just his own flesh and blood. He had an entire race—a race to be proud of.

The term *Black*, which had previously been the greatest insult, was adopted as the name for the race, replacing *colored* or *Negro*. When Stokely Carmichael coined the phrase *Black Power*, he redefined a people and for the first time made the color of their skin a source of pride, and a source of fear among those in the outer society (including other Blacks such as Roy

Wilkins of the NAACP, who felt the phrase set Black Americans back twenty years in their progress in American society). By defusing the term *Black*, Black people defused a great many things that had previously wounded and stigmatized their children and therefore perpetuated mental captivity.

Black people should have defused the word *nigger* while we were at it. When *All in the Family* wanted to use the word, Black organizations protested in an uproar. It was decided *nigger* was too offensive. But *honky* was used constantly on that and other shows. Now *honky* holds no power, but *nigger* can still destroy a child.

During the sixties there was a groundswell of pride and boldness that was infectious and exciting. Walls were crumbling in the larger society, and the fog was clearing in the heads of a generation of Americans. A real freedom was evolving.

Suddenly the world was not simply confined to a twenty-block radius. The world was as large as the planet, and Black Americans had to demand a new place in it, to restructure their boundaries and establish new definitions for themselves.

Television was a phenomenon taking place in every American home. It was exposing real life (and a fantasy life America wanted to be reality) to all of us. While everyone had a television, Black people did not find themselves represented there. For years Black Americans enjoyed *The Andy Griffith Show*, *Father Knows Best*, *Leave It to Beaver*, *American Playhouse*, and the like, but found no Black images. It was obvious that Black America was not in America's imagination. This became an important point for those at the forefront of various Black movements.

There were certainly no Black images that one could consider cool. At this time, if a Black person was on television he or she was definitely *not* cool. It became more and more clear that the system of cool, the system that defined the Black man on the street, was unfamiliar to America, or unacceptable.

This tug-of-war between television's (translation: America's) understanding of cool (translation: Black manhood) and the Black community's understanding of it continues to be fought. At the moment many Blacks are anticipating, and are even beginning to feel, some frustration at the media's attitude toward Michael Jordan, the NBA superstar. While the media deified Magic Johnson—a wonderful guy who, nonetheless, seemed to be a big teenager—it now seems as though the media might begin to tear down Michael Jordan. Michael Jordan is a Black male image that most Black Americans would say is cool (translation: a man—mature, self-assured, sexy, smart, positive). Of course, this manhood—shaped and defined by cool—is contrary to America's idea of how Black men should behave, and so Jordan might be in for trouble. The jury is still out.

This has caused an interesting realization among some Black Americans. America did not know them or did not want to know them. Then television began to make the great division between races and classes crystal clear.

It's important to note that there were many Black Americans who were neither concerned about nor really aware of the lack of Black images on television. They were certainly more willing to enjoy television without Black images than to see television embrace negative, inappropriate, or embarrassing Black images. Television was and is entertainment for these people, and it neither defines nor reflects what they are or should be. These

Black (and white) Americans *define* themselves, and therefore *enjoy* television for what it is.

Back in those days, if it was on television, it was inherently not cool, because television had proven its ignorance of Black people. The consensus was, How can anyone behind the scenes of television know what is truly cool?

This perception was constantly reinforced by television's attempt to capture what it thought was Black reality, or what it thought Black people wished Black reality was. The program *Julia* was a perfect example of television's presentation of Black life. There was a lot of criticism of the show, but Black Americans watched it; after all, here finally was a Black woman, Diahann Carroll, on television. This notion that Blacks watched the show because it had a Black person in it tended to confuse those who produced shows. They began to believe that these images were what Black people wanted to see of themselves. The TV world is very literal—if the ratings are good, give them more of the same.

If television managed to depict something resembling the real symbols of cool, then it was time for those symbols to change; they were in the wrong hands, they are obviously no longer cool.

Television is not truly one-dimensional. Its fantasy world gave us Opie and Andy, whom I loved as a kid. But the *real* world was faithfully delivered every night on the evening news. It may not be a coincidence that the civil rights and liberation movements began to take shape just as everyone was buying their first television set. As a result of the exposure Black reality was getting on the news, the Black community was changing, pledging allegiances, and redefining itself. As the revolution unfolded on the evening news, new Black realities took shape. And as television matured and sought talent wherever it could find it, the real images of cool slowly began to be shown on shows like *Shindig, American Bandstand,* and *Hullabaloo.* The Supremes, the Temptations, Martha and the Vandellas, James Brown, Jr. Walker and the All Stars, Ray Charles, Marvin Gaye, et al., were all displaying real Black people, regular Black people, folks from the ghetto, or from the rural South, or just from hard times. Some of these performers were from solid Black middle-class families with traditional family values, some were from the projects, and some were from single-family homes. The point is that real Black American people were performing on television and were speaking out on the evening news. And Black Americans recognized themselves amongst the diversity of these images.

Although cool was still not being *defined* by television, the images that cool had created were beginning to be *displayed* there.

With so much going on, the definitions of manhood and what a Black man's responsibilities and goals should be were beginning to change. It was no longer enough just to be "bad" on the streets. Now a man had to have knowledge and a unified form of power because, thanks to the television news and the man on a soapbox standing on the corner making speeches, the Black community became more focussed on the fact that the enemy wasn't just a young punk around the corner, he was clearly America and its system.

The fight was now much more complex and therefore required different ammunition. Of course, the battle had always been with the American system, but the common man, the masses, had not usually been in a position to understand or confront it. This would change during the revolution.

The sixties made Black people look at their history—both their African and their American history. Black Americans had to fight their own demons, in the form of conditioned self-hatred. Afros and cornrows became the symbol of self-love and acceptance; dashikis represented an embrace of African heritage; Black English was hailed as a language and African languages and Black studies were taught on college campuses; jazz was finally recognized as America's classical music; and the Beatles and the Stones hailed Black recording artists for their inspiration and instruction. Black people also had to face their memories of captivity and lynchings, as well as continuing violence from the KKK, other racists, and the police.

Black people—the southern Black, the northern Black, the light-skinned, the dark-skinned, the children, the incarcerated, the "ignorant," the brilliant—had to recognize the unity in their struggle. Black men became *brothers*; the women became *sisters*.

In the early sixties Thurgood Marshall and the NAACP had begun challenging the political and judicial system, creating an open path for the many bright young Black people who were ready to enter college. Black people did not all of a sudden become smart during the sixties—it was the beginning of opportunity for these young people, in any real numbers, to enter private, non-Black colleges. Of course, these new steps in American history was not without bloodshed. Medgar Evers, for instance, had to die.

Cool had to expand to accommodate all the new things a young Black man now had to know, understand, and accomplish. Emmett Till, a fourteen-year-old Chicago boy who lost his life in the late fifties, struck a chord for everyone. Here was a young boy brought up with the rules of cool. He was confident and not used to showing fear, even of white people. He was not afraid to say "hey" to a white woman. So, with cool as his guide, he spoke to a white woman in the South. The vicious attack on Emmett Till still rings in the hearts of millions of Black people. His dead body was so mangled that his mother insisted on an open casket so the world could see what America was capable of. On the streets of urban America, the swagger of a cool boy is a front, a facade put on for the benefit of other young boys. It has little honest strength behind it. When three white men felt challenged by it, they were feeling challenged by a Black boy who was trying to become a man. America demonstrated its terror of that possibility by brutally destroying a child.

The Emmett Till incident also demonstrates the fundamental difference between the southern Black and urban Black existence (at least back then). For Blacks the South has always meant, quite literally, life and death. It has traditionally been white America's belly of the beast. *Cool*, as we've seen in the previous chapter, is symbolic. It doesn't survive pure and calculated violence. *Cold* might—and that is perhaps what has developed in urban America today.

Just imagine some of the things going on in America during the sixties. James Brown was singing "I'm Black and I'm Proud," bringing pride and outrage to urban and southerners alike. Angela Davis sported a huge natural and fell in love with George Jackson, a man in prison. With that, Black men in prison were suddenly not criminals, they were "political prisoners." This notion alone required a new way of seeing things, a new way of thinking.

IQ tests were under fire. This previously accepted form of declaring Black people inferior was now being exposed and reformed; why weren't there any questions about how long you should cook chitterlings? Probably because most white Americans didn't cook them.

Jesus was a Black man; is there any doubt left about that? If you went back to the history books, or used the Bible as a document of history and not as merely something to revere, you would ascertain that the color of Jesus's skin was certainly dark. Cleopatra didn't look like Elizabeth Taylor; King Tut was Black; the pyramids were designed and built by Africans. Black Americans came to realize that pride and strength and survival might actually come from their history, their knowledge about themselves and their heritage. Maybe, Black Americans realized, they could survive just by living, and not by fighting each other daily, risking genocide at their own hands.

It was very exciting, very stimulating, and way, way cool. America was on edge and Black America had put it there. A lot of education was going on during this era. The oral tradition was in full force. Everyone was talking, learning, exchanging ideas and information, strengthening each other. Knowledge and intelligence were beginning to head the list of what was considered cool. Knowledge was becoming essential to survival, because the enemy was much bigger than your neighborhood. The battlefield was no longer just your block, it was now these great United States; and the enemy was not just another young Black kid or the KKK, but the silent majority and the Supreme Court. The enemy was the world, and the word, and the mind, and the craziness, and *all* that. The strategy for winning was knowledge and pride.

Because of this awareness and enlightenment, the men of the streets were changing. Cool's limited focus on survival in the streets by challenging yourself with your very life was missing the point. So those rules of cool began to change, to accommodate this new level of understanding that Black men had obtained. For those who still lived with daily violence or poverty, street cool still operated (and will as long as those conditions exist), but Black-on-Black crime smelled of *genocide* and of *conspiracy* (systemic racism began to feel planned rather than arbitrary) and of *self-hatred*, and therefore was becoming more and more uncool. Revolutionary cool, which brought with it a whole new set of symbols, called for knowledge of the world, and of your place in it.

As I've said, a lot of education was going on during this era. Suddenly it became cool to intellectualize. Everyone was talking and learning, exchanging ideas and information. School was still not cool, because it still wasn't to be trusted. But learning—particularly about being Black and descendants of Africans—was very cool. It was no longer shameful to acknowledge the past; captivity, the middle passage, the underground railroad, Marcus Garvey, W. E. B. Du Bois, the renegade and the runaways, and even those who stayed and endured the degradation—all had something to be proud of: strength, endurance, adaptability, intelligence, cunning, determination, perseverance . . .

I recently watched a local show in Minneapolis, a think tank on racism that featured several professionals, mostly women, both Black and white. When the discussion turned to the need for a multicultural educational system, one white panelist pointed out that she knew *many* Blacks who had managed to succeed in life with the traditional one-dimensional education found in public schools. I wanted to shout to her that these Black adults had had the benefit of learning the truth about their own Black American history from the prophets and scholars found on the streets, in the neighborhood bookstores, candy stores, stoops, and sometimes classrooms in the sixties and seventies. They *did* benefit from a multicultural education, but not courtesy of or sanctioned by the U.S. government.

But why was cool changing? What was behind it? Being a child of the Northeast, New York to be exact, my answer will be biased. I'm sure those on the West Coast would say it was because of the Black Panthers. But I would say it was because of Malcolm X.

While cool is a journey, a journey toward manhood, at the end of that journey is a confident, seasoned man whose anger has been harnessed like steam to move things forward. But he does not achieve this confidence until he has had the experiences that bring it. His peers must recognize that he has conquered the obstacles they find themselves faced with, and if he has and he is moving forward, they will have the confidence in him that's required to follow him, and he will have the confidence required to lead. Malcolm X had had those experiences, and while no one knew the details of his life until well after he was famous, his style, manner, and attitude demonstrated that fact. He was not a figurehead whose life experiences were contradictory to his followers. He had been through the streets and was the positive result of that experience. This is why he was beyond cool. He was ultimately the symbol of it.

It is vitally important to note that Malcolm X is not a symbol of the Nation of Islam or the Black Muslims to most Black folks. Malcolm X emerged as a singular voice, a voice that captured tens of thousands of Black people—Christian churchgoers, nonbelievers, the drug-addicted, the educated, capitalists, laborers, the lower, middle, and upper-middle class. Neither Minister Louis B. Farrakhan nor the Nation of Islam have enjoyed the loyalty of the mainstream of Black Americans as Malcolm did. And it is also important to note that Malcolm's pilgrimage to Mecca brought him back to America with the realization that the world's problems were something other than race, that the problem was much more spiritual and moral and that race had simply clouded the issues.

In Malcolm X the personification of street cool was finally available. In the image of Malcolm X and the Panther Party, ultimate Street Cool had been achieved and personified. They were on television, exposed to the masses of Black Americans and menacing the masses of white Americans. America has learned its lesson about putting the Black community's real spokesmen on the news for all to see; doing this fuels their cause by enlightening the country. Now Black leaders like Al Sharpton, whose followers are small in numbers but very vocal, gain the camera's attention, giving the false impression that they speak for the majority of Black people. The Black community has many opinions and political viewpoints, reflective of America's diversity. So it's very difficult today to find leaders who speak for a majority.

As with any image of cool, young Black men adopted the symbols and imitated the style of the many revolutionaries, musicians, and spokesmen of the revolution. Dashikis, red, black, and green flags, posters, berets, and dark sunglasses were everywhere.

While the civil rights movement was gaining momentum and successfully changing the hands of power in the South, the North and urban centers were fighting their own unique struggles. Martin Luther King and members of the Civil Rights movement did not speak to the young Black men of the cities. Simply put, nonviolence was contrary to the dictates of street cool. There was, of course, a deep respect and regard for Martin Luther King and his work among Black Americans everywhere, city or country. But those who lived by the dictates of cool did not find their answer in him. The civil rights movement had no overt aggression, no show of force, no derring-do, no arrogance. Its message of "We shall overcome" did not speak to the anger and fuck-you attitude so integral to cool.

The climate in the South was one in which individual retaliation for injustice was akin to suicide. Confronted with the realities of wide-open spaces and a gun in every home, Black people were more given to complacency. But this complacency was on the outside; inside there was fire. Their anger was released in the churches.

It was through this framework that Martin Luther King and his supporters turned religion into a fighting machine. The Bible became the blueprint for a successful nonviolent effort. It united people while protecting them. Dr. King's ability to make the Bible work against the atrocities of white society and for

Black people made him able to move mountains in the most racist part of the country.

But was it all cool? There might be a need here to talk a bit about the fact that cool is mainly an urban phenomenon, and why. Traditionally, southern Black men have had less of a need for cool than urban Black men. Cool developed as a way for a boy to become a man in an environment where he could not become a man in the traditional way. Also, in crowded cities Black boys are protecting themselves *from each other*, and learning this method of protection from each other.

This is not so in the South. The South's tradition of white violence—lynch mobs, dogs, the KKK—has created another kind of cool, one that is not so individual. The Black southerner's cool is in a quiet unity, a unity which led to the civil rights movement and to the successful exchange of power from white hands to Black. Traditionally southerners are called "country" by northerners and are uniformly considered uncool. It isn't discrimination or snobbery; it's simply that, once again, what makes cool real is the need for it.

Malcolm X was the embodiment of cool. He was a product of the streets, and was a victim of street cool. Obviously, he was so involved in some aspects of street cool that he wound up in prison. But Malcolm displayed the ultimate purpose of cool: He survived. He survived the streets by remaining healthy; and then he not only survived prison, but persevered.

Malcolm X made both knowledge and religion cool. It was in prison that Malcolm became a self-taught scholar. He embraced the Muslim religion and joined the Nation of Islam. And when he came out of prison he became a spokesman for that religion and for the inherent beauty and strength of Black people.

Religion became cool—or, more accurately, *his* religion became cool. It was still not cool to be religious, and certainly not to be a Christian who touted a God alien to those adhering to the rules of street cool. Malcolm introduced the streets to a Black religion, a religion with a Black prophet and a Black leader. He was brilliant and eloquent, quietly angry and infinitely wise and fearless. He talked about the "blue-eyed devil" and taking what's yours "by any means necessary," and preached that if you gotta go, "take five of them with you."

He fascinated whites and frightened them at the same time. On one occasion Malcolm was interviewed on the streets by a reporter. After asking Malcolm a question, the reporter turned to a neatly dressed Black man and asked his opinion. His opinion was directly counter to the pro-Black Power opinion Malcolm had just delivered. Rather than debate this man, Malcolm laughed. He then said, directly, conversationally, that only when a Black man is interviewed will the press have another Black man standing nearby who will counter what he's had to say. Malcolm was never intimidated and he never defended himself. He embodied Black manhood, as it had developed in the streets of this country. And he was embraced in turn.

Malcolm and the Nation were also embraced because of their quite tangible influence. During the sixties, Black communities were plagued with drug addicts and crime. Heroin was the drug of choice, and young people were hooked. They stole from their mothers and grandmothers. They nodded out on corners and begged for money from children. Inevitably they wound up in prison. But when they returned, they had been reborn. It was a miracle. The miracle didn't come from the heavens, or from Jesus, it came from the Nation of Islam. In prison many young men embraced the religion and its teachings. Self-sufficiency, self-pride, a sense of family, a philosophy of owning your own business, home, church—these were the tenets of the Black Muslim movement. The Muslim religion's ability to rehabilitate Black men in prison still exists today. It seems the religion has been a haven, and perhaps a protector, behind prison walls. While most Black people did not adopt the Muslim religion, Malcolm and the Nation were considered cool because they seemed to embody everything cool was set out to do, while creating a new level of manhood and maturity among those in the streets.

In New York a valuable TV program, Gil Noble's *Like It Is*, continually explores the issues facing Black Americans. On one program devoted to Malcolm X, a Black man gave a tearful final statement: "Malcolm offered the opportunity for me to be a man in this country." It was a powerful moment to watch, and it echoed the sentiments expressed in the eulogy at Malcolm X's funeral given by Ossie Davis. It helps one to realize that men who live in an aggressive and dangerous environment cannot be asked to be meek when fighting for their lives. Since the country did not understand that, cool had to.

While Malcolm spoke to the urban centers and the Panthers spoke to the West Coast and college students, there was another group of Black men who had become symbols of success, images of another style of cool, and highly visible on television. They are the Black athletes.

Athletes are traditionally apolitical. However, the rise of the

Black athlete during the sixties was not without politics. These young men were well aware of the revolution, and although they had channeled their anger in another direction and survived the streets (if they had been members of the streets to begin with), they recognized their importance as images of Black manhood and refused to compromise their manhood for the sake of the sport or the money. Needless to say, athletes are usually considered very cool; after all, cool is survival, success, strength, confidence. Athletes rarely need to "front" their cool, because they can prove it through their sport. And the athletes of the revolution did not disappoint. While Walt Frazier and Earl Monroe symbolized the old street cool, Muhammad Ali (Cassius Clay, remember?), Kareem Abdul Jabbar (Lew Alcindor, remember?), and the Olympic runners Tommie Davis and John Carlos, who raised their fists while the anthem played, brought the revolution to sports.

The world was changing and expanding, and cool had to expand its definitions. Of course, cool is not a living, breathing thing. It is a style of living, a way of identifying and defining manhood. But as the world changes, manhood must change as well. Religion, knowledge, and politics had to be included in the new definition of cool.

Although every stage of cool offers its positive avenues, it offers its negative avenues as well. In the streets, cool can lead to drugs; with the revolution, cool can lead to the kidnapping of Patty Hearst, to Stokely Carmichael making what he considered the ultimate statement of manhood when he said the Black woman's place in the revolution is "prone," and to the death and destruction of important men, and with them brilliant ideas.

As Black men embraced the symbols and images of this new cool, they felt the need to define their new manhood and to redefine the Black woman's role in the community. The Black woman's best place was prone, Stokely had said. This statement, and the images presented by the Panthers and others, gave the young Black man a sense that the Black woman had to be suppressed. As he took his position as the warrior, she had to sit down and shut up.

The revolution, and its symbols and styles of cool, caused an almost permanently destructive turn for Black male-and-female relationships. It had been conveyed to the young Black man that he'd relinquished control to the Black woman. Whites would hire a Black woman because she was "less threatening," so she became a better breadwinner; or she bought into the American way of life and therefore was less "rebellious" or resistant, and so was more accepted; or she joined the church and was less apt to fall prey to drugs and alcohol. For a variety of reasons, the Black woman was perceived as running the race. Anyone who has a Black father or boyfriend or brother knows damn well that the Black man is far from being controlled by his woman. Still, the myth was perpetuated, and went even further. He had become emasculated because she had gotten out of control.

It's my feeling that this was the beginning of a campaign against Black women that has insinuated itself into today's rap lyrics. It's a sad state of affairs to have to listen to popular Black songs—that you *know* teenaged Black girls are snapping their fingers to—which call a girl "poison," and brags that the singer and his crew "used to do her."

The image of the traditional Black family with a balance of power and responsibilities was somehow rejected and is now lost to many young men. Because cool, and their manhood, is so caught up in symbols, masses of young Black men began imitating what they saw and what was conveyed. The image of the domineering Black woman was perpetuated, and young Black men were empowered by the images of cool and manhood put forth by the revolutionaries. While the revolution's rhetoric deified Black women for the first time—"the darker the berry, the sweeter the juice,"—it also told young Black men to "put them in their place."

Cool was turning *cold*.

This essay explains some of the confusion:

The Values of Manhood by Manning Marable

In a racist, sexist, class-divided society, the Black man's struggle for self-discovery is fraught with detours and difficulty. For me, this odyssey has meant challenging the values I held as a young man.

I grew up in a Black, middle-class suburban household in the sixties. From my father I absorbed the values of hard work, independence and determination. From my mother I learned the value of spiritual strength and the blessing of caring for others and gained a passion for scholarship and writing. I learned in this secure environment that life is rational and predictable; knowledge is power, and any problems can be overcome by analysis and hard work.

My young male peers held other stereotypes about what it means to be a "successful Black male." A strong Black man never shows his feelings. He is assertive, opinionated and imminently self-confident.

This cardboard characterization of "manhood" was unfortunately popularized in the sixties by academics and activists alike. In college we students read Daniel Patrick Moynihan's controversial "Moynihan's Report," which placed the blame for the disintegration of the Black family and the "castration" of Black males on the Black woman. From the streets, our generation of young Black men learned that one very prominent Black nationalist even asserted that the only position for women within his organization was "prone." Although the crudely blatant sexism of these attitudes and remarks always turned me off, like most young African-American males I absorbed many of their assumptions.

My reconstruction began in 1974, with my appointment to the faculty of the all-women's Smith College in Massachusetts. There I became friends with several articulate and brilliant women. Johnnetta Cole, then a professor of anthropology at the University of Massachusetts, was like an older sister, inviting me into her home and shaping my nascent political ideas. The poet Sonia Sanchez inspired me to write; educator Johnnella Butler challenged me to understand the role of culture in political life. From these relationships came the powerful recognition that Black women's experiences had produced a set of values and perceptions that challenges stereotypes. They understand the oppression of sexual discrimination and the importance of making connections between the dynamics of race and gender. Sisters have taught me that we should listen to the poetry within, capture and express our inner beauty as part of our political and social being. The nexus of beauty, warmth and strength within Black women taught me to redefine any understanding of power and social change.

In recent years, my life moved in new and unexpected directions. My relationship with my wife came apart as we grew in opposite directions personally and politically. I was struck with a chronic illness, sarcoidosis, which forced me to rethink my entire life and its meaning. I became determined to go beyond merely interpreting Black history and the political world. Instead, I decided to accept a challenging position at Columbia University to implement my ideas into practice by building the Institute for Research in African-American Studies.

In the process, once again, I relied on the intelligence, hard work, and insights of Black women. Daria Oliver, my executive assistant, and Cheri McLeod-Pearcey, my executive secretary, have helped to expand our program and to build an academic enterprise that may one day impact Black America in a lasting manner. My Black female graduate assistants, including Monique Williams and Johanna Fernandez, are organizing conferences and conducting detailed research on the Black experience.

But my most significant relationship is with an extraordinary woman of rare intellect and beauty, Leith Mullings. As Professor of Anthropology at the Graduate Center of the

City University of New York, Leith has long fought for the interests of Black folk. Her scholarship in urban and medical anthropology, combined with her personal political involvement in Harlem and New York's Black community, provides a model which any intellectual worthy of the title would want to emulate. She has a gift of being able to relate to people of all classes, backgrounds, and educational abilities. Leith and I are working on a theory of Black America in the post–Civil Rights era. She has taught me that the finest scholarship must be linked to the practical struggle for empowerment of our people.

I'm convinced that the Black man will only reach his fullest potential when he learns to draw upon the strengths and insights of the Black woman. We must challenge the sexism embedded within our popular music, our culture, and our institutions. Sisters have tried to tell us for years that "manhood" cannot be measured in material acquisitions, or by a set of mainstream, middle-class criteria not designed with us in mind. Being proud and comfortable in our heritage and culture—achieving despite racism, sexism, and any other obstacles that the system has placed before us— is the best way to achieve both Black womanhood and manhood.

Reprinted by permission of the author.

chapter three

Middle-Class Cool

"We're a winner,
and never let anybody say
you can't make it
'cause a feeble mind is in your way.

No more tears will we cry,
and we have finally dried our eyes.
And we're movin' on up
Movin' on up.
Lord, have mercy,
we're movin' on up.

And we're living proof

and all's alert

that we're true

from the good black dirt.

And we're a winner.

And everybody knows the truth.

We just keep on pushin',

like your leaders tell you to.

Curtis Mayfield, 1967

"Ain't no stoppin' us now."

McFadden and Whitehead, 1979

the songs of the sixties and seventies tell the whole story. There were so many positive songs to choose from it was ridiculous. But if anyone reflected and amplified the voice of Chicago's inner city it was Curtis Mayfield. I desperately miss Curtis Mayfield. His tragic accident sure does make you wonder. His smooth, kind, intelligent lyrics and voice calmed the fears and tempers of folks as they carved their piece of the proverbial pie. He was making a comeback in the early nineties when his staging collapsed, and he is now a quadriplegic. Why is it that all the positive voices get snuffed out in their prime in this country?

Getting a piece of that pie was certainly something to sing about. During the seventies some Blacks were able to tune up their vocal chords. In the years following the turbulent sixties, many Blacks reached a level where they could be considered middle and upper-middle class, the loose criteria for this status ranging from one's income (over $35,000 for a family of four living in a utopian rural town without television or a Toys "R" Us), to education (college graduate at least), to lifestyle (a person who hangs out with educated, well-heeled Americans yet whose bank account is itself not that impressive), and background (in the upper classes through parentage).

Of course there is a huge Black lower class that defines the higher classes simply as money—if you have it, you're a member; if you don't, you're not. After the sixties there was a growing Black community that had it. And therefore there was a *need* for a new definition of what it meant to be cool. Once again, cool had to change and adapt to a new reality for Black people.

The Tradition of Money

Middle-class cool is a new phenomenon. In fact, just twenty years ago the two terms were in total contradiction. Since cool came from the Black man's struggle to survive on the streets, the middle-class lifestyle was completely incompatible with the need to be cool.

Prior to the revolution the Black community enjoyed economic diversity. There were families living in the community with two parents who worked—sometimes for the city or federal government or as teachers or businesses owners. There were Blacks who were plagued with poverty—single parents, welfare recipients, whatever. There were those who were professionals, with private offices down the block—doctors, dentists, lawyers, accountants, etc. For the most part the diversity was very homogeneous.

But among those with some level of financial success was a healthy amount of Uncle Toms. There were the lawyers with a greasy stocking cap hanging behind the bathroom door because they flattened their hair every night to control their natural kinkiness and thus be more palatable to whites, or those light-skinned salesclerks who chose to mingle strictly with whites, or the Blacks who mimicked whites and truly believed that "white was right." In those days, in order to better themselves some Blacks adopted a "yessum" attitude and played up to white people in the hopes of being accepted, because that acceptance sometimes brought work, money, and a better life.

If these "yessums" achieved enough financial success to leave the Black community, they did. But if they had to remain there the people in their community eventually recognized their attitude, and they suffered from hostility and isolation.

Most of these Uncle Toms felt that the animosity shown them by other Blacks was simply due to jealousy. To some degree this was true—poorer people do tend to be jealous of people who have. Since most poor Blacks didn't see a possibility of ever achieving any level of financial success, at least not through America's conventional methods, there was some jealousy. Yet if offered the opportunity to achieve financial success in the way their neighbors had, they would decline.

Prior to the seventies, many less fortunate Blacks perceived other Blacks as compromising in order to attain success, and were unwilling to compromise themselves in that way.

Compromise, however, is in the eye of the beholder. We can't define it but we know it when we see it. It is and always has been a volatile and explosive issue. If a doorman tips his hat and says "sir" and "madam," has he compromised himself too much? Compromise became a gray area. There are those purists in the community (who also tend to be racial bullies) who can define the word so narrowly that you are forced to stay *put* in order to stay *Black*.

This perception of animosity toward compromise had its roots in aspects of the captive experience. Malcolm, Du Bois, and Dr. John Henrik Clarke, among others, in speaking of the *house Negro* and the *field Negro* phenomenon, exposed a taboo that had been with Black Americans for generations.

House Negroes were the captives the master allowed to work in his home, while field Negroes were those who toiled the land. Needless to say, the house Negro received a great deal more hands-on (if not formal) education. These Negroes were often caught in the middle and sometimes found themselves ostracized, mistrusted, or misunderstood by Blacks in the field. But there were house Negroes who gained access to important information, such as who was being sold or punished or what was going on inside the "big house," which was then passed on to other captives. There were also those who, because they could read and write, would provide information from newspapers to other captives or write passes for those who escaped.

These were the same people who were able to get table scraps to their relatives or other loved ones. In other words, some of them maintained loyalties to the other captives. But there were many who began to accept and adopt the master's point of view about the Black man's station in life.

Enter Uncle Thomas

It was this type of captive who brought about the stereotype of the Uncle Tom. This middleman may have been the forefather of a middle-class Black who had a modicum of financial success but who was embarrassed by his own race. Sometimes called "handkerchief heads," because they wore handkerchiefs to keep the hair plastered nice and straight (one of those little compromises), these middlemen were not respected by other Blacks and often felt their disdain. Sometimes, as a reaction to this disenfranchisement from his people, the Uncle Tom first acted superior, then eventually convinced himself of his superiority to those Blacks who were financially below him.

Quiet as it's kept, there were many successful Black folks back then who were not Toms. These were the ones who pioneered certain fields and achieved their positions through hard work and without compromise. They were proud of their color and felt they were a symbol of what Blacks could achieve. Ultimately, they made it more and more obvious that the Uncle Tom had another path to success.

Another reason that Uncle Toms are considered uncool is that they are ignorant of their true position in America. Uncle Toms somehow imagine that if they deny their color long enough or well enough, they will be completely accepted into

American society. Racism makes this notion not only laughable but impossible. But it isn't just racism that makes this scheme unworkable. It's the fact that most white Americans feel just as uncomfortable with Uncle Toms as other blacks do, and for the very same reasons. America as a whole is beginning to know uncool when it sees it. And thanks to the enlightenment that went on in the revolutionary sixties, ignorance of yourself as a Black person has become unacceptable, and uncool.

The Blacks who struggled through life in the streets of America's cities may have felt envy for the possessions others had, but they made a conscious decision to accept the fact that they didn't and wouldn't have it. The prevailing feeling was, "If I had so-and-so's money I would still be cool; I wouldn't be so uppity." But there was no such thing back then as having money *and* being cool. The means of getting so-and-so's money would null-and-void your cool almost immediately. Or, better said, cool would null-and-void your ability to attain money back then, and justifiably so.

But for many this conscious acceptance has turned into defiance, and it is this element of the street personality that frustrates, infuriates, and confounds Americans—Black and white. What began as genuine rejection of becoming an Uncle Tom, of selling out, may have become for many an ingrained lifestyle, and subsequently may have created a poverty class who no longer has that excuse but has come to accept and operate within a poverty mentality.

Presumed within being cool is a discernible self-respect and self-pride. In America, a Black person was not yet free enough to see himself as anything except Black first—except the Uncle Tom. The most powerful characteristic operating in an Uncle

Tom is self-hatred or self-denial, *self* being defined as one's Blackness.

A new Tom exists, but the delineation is graying. Is Clarence Thomas a Tom or is he simply a pioneer, a true conservative who feels Black Americans should hold themselves to the same standards as all Americans and that they should blame *themselves* for their plight, or better yet, not blame at all, but just get on with it? Justice Thomas is an extreme example, but he does demonstrate the confusion. There are many Blacks who feel shackled by the politics of being Black. The conservative notion is not all bad. But Justice Thomas double-crossed himself when he pulled out, as if from a hat, one of America's most horrendous racial crimes—lynching—in order to shame Congress and thus save himself. He did the classic Tom two-step—embrace his Blackness when it's convenient and embrace white conservative ideals when that better serves him. He also seemed to be advised too much by others, and thus was perceived as not being his own man, and therefore not cool. Finally, the information the media supplied about his behavior toward his sister—who was a single mother on welfare—was reminiscent of those unfortunate few who feel "We got ours, now you get yours," without acknowledging the help they received from those Blacks who were hosed and bitten by dogs to pave the way for their educational opportunities.

Perhaps the biggest change in cool for streetwise Blacks as they began to make money was their definition of "Blackness."

Being cool was contrary to being middle class for a hundred years after the Civil War. We all know there was a misconception that Blacks were lazy, rebellious, or ignorant and did not want to succeed. What has been ignored, unrecognized, or misunderstood was the tradition of the middle-class Black who made his money from bowing and scraping—not just to white America, but more likely to the very members of white America who were the most oppressive during captivity.

Black America recognizes that white America's middle class was made up of struggling, embittered folks who hated Blacks more than America's upper class did. The overseer—that pathetic, angry, and enslaved soul caught between the aristocracy and the captive—was often the obstacle to upward mobility for Blacks. In the days of captivity, to bow and scrape to this wretched soul was unforgivable. So, with arrogance, a huge class of Black folks who struggled with the poverty and dangers of America's streets refused to join the ranks of those willing to tap-dance for the overseer in hopes of earning a living.

The Privileged Few

Rich Blacks are not alien to the Black community. There was always a large group of successful Black professionals in America. In some instances captivity played a role in this world of fourth- and fifth-generation Black professionals, and it is no coincidence that many of them are light-skinned.

During the antebellum period white people of the Old South kept, raped, and often fell in love with and married Blacks. Those who chose to, out of either pride or embarrassment, would send the offspring of this union up north or to Europe to be educated. This gave rise to a large population of lighter-skinned Blacks with a long tradition of receiving a higher education. These were the professionals who service the Black community during Jim Crow and segregation.

The members of this society maintained much of the Black wealth and privilege for decades, before the civil rights and Black Power movements brought the more disadvantaged Black families into America's system of higher education.

There was also the tradition of the intelligent and darker-skinned Black male who attended Howard University, became a doctor, engineer, dentist . . . and quickly married a "high yella" Black woman. There were many reasons for this; although some fell in love on campus just like any red-blooded American male, others simply wanted "pretty" children with "good" hair, while others wanted the trophy of a "yella" girl on his arm. Many college-educated Black girls were lighter-skinned and some men simply wanted a wife who could uplift him and would introduce him and their children to finer things. Traditionally it was perceived that the college-educated light-skinned Black woman had the benefit of a more refined upbringing and was better equipped for life in the upper-middle class. Whichever the reason, a fairer-skinned upper class prevailed.

A very light-skinned, big-boned, handsome man I once dated was about fourth-generation college-educated and came from a long line of dentists. His dark-skinned grandfather, now a retired dentist and a self-satisfied man, anguished over his grandson's decision to become a musician. He lectured his grandson for ten minutes during one visit: "Look at you—you a pretty boy. That's why I married your grandmother, so you'd be a pretty boy. And look what you've done with it. Nothin'." All the women in his family were light-skinned, and all the men were successful.

There were those Blacks who had become successful as a result of segregation—if you can't go to the white dentist you have to go to the Black one; if you can't eat at the white lunch counter you've got to go to the Black one. Some of these successful Blacks regarded other Blacks in the same way whites regarded them—as a group to disassociate yourself from.

Since cool is something anointed by your peers, this group of Blacks was completely shut out of the system of cool. Since it is a system devised by young Black males to establish their own manhood in the face of the dangers of the streets, this class— whose children were raised in a more traditional American way—was not considered cool by those who needed that system.

Light-skinned Blacks were certainly not the only financially successful Black people. There were shopkeepers, ministers, liquor store owners, contractors, handymen, and so on, of every hue. For the most part though, these folks made up the Black middle class and were not counted among the professional or privileged class.

And, not to be forgotten, there was always the gangster class: the numbers runners, the bookies—the *opportunists*.

This skeleton in Black America's closet, of class consciousness through color consciousness, had to be exposed during the revolutionary sixties, because it was the descendants of these groups—the privileged, the house Negro, the field Negro, and all of those in between—who would finally come head-to-head when the clarion call of "Free your mind" rang in the fifties, sixties, and seventies.

Makin' Money
the Hard Way

There was a new group of people who were neither gangsters, Toms, nor Jacks and Jills. (Jack and Jill is the name of a social club developed by the privileged class. When successful Black couples moved to the white suburbs their children grew up in all-white communities. The parents panicked—their children needed other Blacks! So they started a club where Black children of privilege could meet other Black children. Needless to say, the club became very exclusive and gained a reputation for being snobbish. Rumors prevailed that you couldn't join unless your skin was lighter than the color of a paper bag. This club perpetrated separatism of the classes, and might not have proved racially beneficial in the way the families originally envisioned. Black was their skin color, or their heritage, but their isolation kept them from really experiencing what it meant to be Black in America. Many of them suffered during the turbulent sixties as they came face-to-face—often on college campuses—with Blacks from the streets.) This new group of Blacks were making money and were very cool by street cool definitions. These folks enjoyed the loyalty, enthusiasm and collective pride of the Black community—particularly those living in the ghetto. These were the folks under the direction of Berry Gordy.

Motown was showing the world real Black people. These Black Americans were unencumbered by the politics of race. They were talented and positive. Berry Gordy may have made sure their image was palatable enough for all of America to digest, but that was okay with the fans, who were basically un-aware that he was doing so. Black Americans who had lived in the ghetto believed strongly in looking good (an essential part of being cool), so it was perfect that the mighty Temptations, the Four Tops, the Supremes, and the Miracles always "vined" (a *really* old term for being well dressed). The sharper the out-fit, the more these performers demonstrated that they came from the streets and were proud of it. Motown, James Brown, Aretha Franklin, Little Anthony and the Imperials, et al., showed the way on how to succeed yet remain indisputably cool. Berry Gordy seemed to know the community well. He of-fered mainstream America Diana Ross and the Supremes, the Temptations, and the Jackson Five; but while Black America enjoyed those ultrasmooth groups, they also enjoyed the ones who were just a little rougher, like Martha and the Vandellas, the Four Tops, and Marvin Gaye.

The possibility of achieving monetary success and respect while remaining true to being cool was proudly demonstrated by many recording artists of the fifties, sixties, and seventies. Berry Gordy demonstrated how successful you could be in business while remaining cool. He also demonstrated that Black American talent was worth a lot of money.

Movin' On Up
(Lord, Have Mercy)

Indulge me, okay? If street cool is cool in its infancy, and rev-olutionary cool is in adolescence, then middle-class cool is cool becoming an adult. Within each mode of cool thus far, individ-ual maturity develops in various ways. But all Black Americans have gone through certain stages of development that can be chronicled through cool.

The revolution was a time of self-discovery and self-love. Previous to the revolution, Black history had been taught by those who did not want to portray the truth accurately. Consequently the idea of Black inferiority spread like an infection. Some Black folks tried not to be Black: lightening their skin, straightening their hair, speaking as properly as possible—the whole nine yards. But the revolution and civil rights movement taught Black Americans about their beauty, their illustrious history, the beauty of their mother country. King Tut and other pharaohs, the Sphinx (whose broad flat nose is mysteriously missing), Nefertiti, and so many more were confirmed as being African. Nikki Giovanni made sure everyone celebrated their Blackness.

This sense of pride and unity helped to provide strength and power. This knowledge, coupled with the tactics of the civil rights movement and the Black Power struggle, and perhaps even fueled by America's anger, disillusionment, and guilt over the murder of John F. Kennedy, forced America to open its doors, beginning with its educational institutions.

Since freedom and enslavement are mostly in the mind—the concepts aren't imaginary, but they're perpetuated there—the real power of racism is to get you to enslave yourself. Honest education was about to make a profound impact.

Cool was changing once again. It had guided young Black boys through the streets and through the revolution, and now it would help see them through college. The rules had to change again. Style, attitude, ability to defend—or to seem as though you could—served no real purpose on campus, but were still very much a part of the young male's awareness. These rules still operated on the streets for young boys, but not for the young men at Amherst, Yale, Duke, Stamford, UCLA, Dartmouth, Syracuse, Trinity, Franklin and Marshall, et al,. who were faced with new obstacles.

Survival had a very different meaning for them. There was a need to succeed in college academically, a need to pursue a career, and a need to function within society—this was what the struggle had been about. But thanks to the enlightenment of the sixties, the most important need was to survive as a Black man, and not just a man. These pioneers had quite a strange frontier to conquer. Essentially they had to design the way for a Black male to become an American man *and* remain true to his Blackness, as defined within the context of cool.

During the seventies, cool became a subtle, spiritual guide, a "correctness" within the soul and with the *community* (or, for today's young Black male, the 'hood). The struggle to remain cool was very internal. Ultimately cool became his conscience.

If the desire to remain cool had died or become obsolete, Black America would have failed itself, and in turn America would have failed at incorporating Black people into the mainstream. If these young Black men had abandoned their need to be cool at this time in America, they would have become useless to those who were left behind, and to the generation who came before them—who had lived through the fire hoses and dogs, and who wanted and needed for their children to succeed. These young men would have ended up as just another group of Toms, and there were already too many of them. Needless to say, this dedication to remaining cool with the community while achieving in the white world and by the white world's standards caused major conflicts.

In the late sixties and early seventies young, intelligent, enlightened Black men and women strutted onto college campuses. Now, face-to-face with white America's kids, and partaking of America's educational secrets on sprawling campuses with the best facilities and intellectual competition, young Black men and women were having to redefine cool and themselves as Black people. Being cool was no longer just about being a *man* on the block.

One of the most threatening aspects of this experience—the thing that caused the greatest need for a new cool—was the fact that all of a sudden a Black male's development was no longer measured by those on the block.

The social atmosphere—the new neighborhood—was filled with different measuring sticks. In some ways, in trying to behave according to these new standards so as to be considered a "man" by his new peers, he was threatening his own "manhood," the manhood that *his* environment recognized. And he risked being ostracized and feeling emasculated.

My friend Ed, a bright, attractive, athletic young Black man, tried for three consecutive years to get into medical school. He worked as a lab technician at a major New York hospital and helped write research papers, hobnobbed with the administrators, studied, and reapplied. Our friendship was tumultuous because of the pressures of his trying to get into medical school. His reasons for not being selected rarely had anything to do with grades or abilities. Ed would return from interviews with white admissions officers and tell me about what this "white man" wanted him to do. "He wanted me to walk like a white man, to grin and smile all the time, to be grateful to him. I couldn't take it. Forget it. If I can't be myself then I won't be a doctor." If I tried to suggest that maybe he was just perceiving it that way, I became a target. "You want me to act white, too. You're always on the white man's side anyway."

Of course he got into medical school, one of the top institutions in the country. While in the mostly white school, his perceptions have changed, although very slowly. It wasn't until his final year that he was able to ease up at all. By then he was different—a lot more "American," a lot less suspicious, and therefore a lot more acceptable and promotable.

He explained it to me this way, after all was said and done: "Black men are going crazy out here trying to deal with this shit." And that's about all the explanation we'll ever get. At thirty-eight years old, Ed is finally considering getting married. Previous to that, the emotional turmoil of race made his relationships impossible. And, no, he doesn't walk any differently.

Blacks who grew up in the streets of America's cities entered colleges, high schools, and elementary schools filled with whites of privilege. But these schools were filled with Blacks of privilege as well, Blacks whose families had attended college for generations.

Many Blacks, particularly those in the North and Midwest who were members of the privileged class, had been safe and insulated for decades. Some of these Jacks and Jills were suddenly forced to deal with a very diverse representation of their own people. Some of them were awakened to their Blackness and their history because of this; others were already awake thanks to television and occasionally because of the blessing of enlightened parents.

A good friend from an upper-class Black family attended Harvard University in the early seventies. He told me a couple of funny stories about his alma mater. One was that whenever a white person asked him what school he attended he would answer, "Harvard" and, after a pause, the white person would say, "Oh, Howard, of course." I love that story. It's typical of the daily bullshit Blacks put up with; small, subtle, annoying bullshit. And if you react you're a "nigga with an attitude."

The other story is also important. This one involved a conversation he'd had with a couple of fellow Black freshmen back in 1971. In discussing what it was like being enrolled at Harvard, his classmates were acting real cocky about it. My friend got annoyed and asked them how they thought they managed to be going to Harvard. One of them replied, "Because I am very intelligent and I kicked ass on the boards." My friend looked at them and said, "Listen, you ain't the first smart niggas in this world. You're here because a lot of Black people got their asses kicked in Watts and Mississippi so you could be here. Don't forget that."

I must add that many of my friends relayed stories during this time of their lives about white people asking them where they went to college. When they answered Harvard, Princeton, Smith, MIT, Northwestern, Stanford, Brown, whatever, the white folks would say something that implied that these young Black people must be very grateful for this opportunity. None of us were grateful to white people for the opportunity to attend colleges we'd deserved to attend for generations. But many of us were grateful to those folks who preached, who marched, who got lynched, who joined hands, who were humiliated, and who gave their lives so that we could go to these colleges. America has to remember that, and it must realize that the loyalty and indebtedness young Black people felt and feel toward those who paved the way, and *who never even benefited themselves from their efforts,* runs deep—deeper than any gratitude to white people, liberal or otherwise, for America's slow and often insignificant changes.

A host of enlightened, confident, and diverse young Black people emerged from these college experiences as eager, intelligent adults who were ready to take on the corporate world and ready to make money. Some found themselves in suits, behind desks, with a corporate image to uphold, earning good money, and doing it nine-to-five. *Cool* made them check themselves out. *What would the community think of how we're behaving?* That's hard to shake. Those who didn't care what the community thought missed the whole point of the revolution.

Just to give an example, it was once rumored that Billy Dee Williams wondered if the Black community liked him or thought he was a joke. His success had so removed him that he wasn't sure how the "folks" perceived him. He was being portrayed as a heartthrob; as a smooth, cool dude (every generation gets *one*; Denzel Washington is Hollywood's handsome leading Black man right now). But he was so removed from the community that he had no sense of how he was perceived by his audience. As an actor, this was important to his career. As a Black man in America, this was important to his emotional survival. But, it was *only* a rumor.

There should come a time when a man no longer cares if he is cool. The catch-22 is that you are never really cool, never really a mature man, until you no longer care if you're cool (translated: you no longer care what others think). But it is not safe for a Black man to reject cool too soon; he runs the risk of losing touch with the reality of America.

A friend who was about thirty-two years old told me about walking on a deserted block one night near his home in New York City. A young Black guy who looked a bit sinister, maybe because the teenager had on the stereotypical hooded sweatshirt, sneakers, and jeans, was walking toward him. My friend says he felt that familiar adrenaline rush and prepared himself to kick ass if he had to, because he thought the guy might want to rip him off or something. Suddenly my friend heard a new voice in his head. It told him, "Wait, what are you doing? Why are you preparing to fight—just to show this guy he can't take you off? This guy could kill you or something." My friend decided to turn around and walk toward an open store. He then told me, "I was risking my life so I wouldn't look soft to this guy. Then I realized, Who cares what that kid thinks of me? My life is more important than that." Needless to say, my friend probably *is* considered soft by this kid. On the streets, he's no longer cool. But he no longer lives on the streets, and therefore has no need to abide by its rules. And, in all fairness, the kid was probably an A student on his way home, scared and tired.

The point, though, is that when a man knows he's cool—with himself—he is free to let cool go. But he mustn't let go too soon. Imagine the young Black man who made it out of the streets because of the racial pride provided by Malcolm X, the defiance of the Black Panthers, the humor of Dick Gregory, the self-sufficiency of the Muslims, the moral righteousness of Martin Luther King, and the hard work and determination of his family—imagine him arriving on campus or getting a job and "becoming white," ignoring the importance of being cool with the neighborhood.

With the influx of Blacks into America's colleges, white America's children were no more prepared for the racial diversity than were some of Black America's children. Their ignorance, coupled with the legacy of self-righteousness of the hippie movement and in many cases their own out-and-out racism and hostility, created a volatile "getting to know you" period.

The white private colleges, in general, had no support system in place for its Black students. The "mixers," the school newspapers, the literary magazines, the student government, and the entire social systems were still operating in their traditional ways. Often the Black students had to tackle many issues besides just getting good grades.

One example of the conflicts on campus occurred in the late eighties when I started my own business. Unfortunately, this incident reflects America's shift to a more conservative viewpoint, since it happened at Columbia University—a "bastion of liberalism."

I worked part-time at Columbia. During that period there was a serious racial conflict on campus involving Black freshmen. At first it was dismissed as spring fever. But once school officials began to take the problem seriously, they chose to perceive its cause as the fact that Black students did not know how to mingle on campus because of the segregation of the eighties—young Black students had for the most part attended all-Black high schools and therefore were not comfortable on white campuses, which was leading to many misunderstandings. Eventually it occurred to Black students that young white students had *also* attended segregated schools, lived in segregated neighborhoods, and received a segregated curriculum that taught them nothing about Black culture and history, which of course is American culture and history, other than slavery. White Americans were afflicted with the same isolationist disease; they also did not know how to relate.

Back in the late sixties and early seventies, exposure to this lifestyle created new value systems. For some of those first-generation college-educated Blacks the conflicts of race, racism, the revolution, and white America's educational system posed an internal problem. They were even more profoundly aware now that a traditional American education was very important. Therefore, raising a family began to have a different price tag on it; public education was no longer a desirable option, since many Blacks had now experienced the vast difference between public and private schooling (or, for that matter, between a public education in the Black community and a public education in the white community—a difference to which I can attest firsthand).

The Black neighborhoods were still filled with many of the same dangers as before, so it was time to seek refuge in the suburbs. Streetwise Blacks who had previously ostracized other Blacks with these attitudes and values were now finding themselves with these same feelings. Suddenly everybody was becoming "middle class," and acceptance of this label came with the status itself.

But there was a difference. This group of middle-class Blacks felt they had achieved this status through the cries of "Black Power" and "We shall overcome." Many felt they were not a contradiction of these issues, but the result. Finally, there was no guilt, no fear, no insecurities, and no shame about their history or their color.

The first Black Power struggles had given many of these newly middle-class folks a pride in themselves as Black people—a pride in their spirit—which allowed them a confidence and self-esteem that no previous generation had enjoyed. Blatant racism did not penetrate, but infinitely more important, subtle racism was now more easily identifiable and thus could be either ignored or confronted. Ultimately, choice is power, and many Black people began to understand that having a choice about anything in life is both liberating and powerful.

With a constant awareness of the continuing struggle, many newly arrived middle-class Blacks carved a place for themselves, both physically and emotionally, somewhere between white America and the streets of America. And they had no intentions of going back. These Blacks took advantage of the doors that were forced open, and they would be damned if they wouldn't be allowed to enjoy some of what this country had to offer—without the stigma of being an Uncle Tom.

So again, out of necessity, a new cool emerged—middle-class cool—an intricate combination of being a Black man and part of America's corporate and academic environments. This new middle class is streetwise *and* book-smart. This combination is a blessing and a curse. With an awareness of the struggle and a dedication to their roots, the new middle class is in constant conflict—playing the game but hating the rules.

Enter the Backlash

The Gender *Divide*
BLACK WOMEN'S GAINS IN CORPORATE AMERICA OUTSTRIP BLACK MEN'S

THAT RAISES SOME CONCERNS BOTH ON AND OFF THE JOB; WHITE BOSSES PLAY A PART

TAUGHT TO BE A CHAMELEON

These headlines appeared on the front page of the *Wall Street Journal* on March 8, 1994. The clipping was sent to me by a white editor friend of mine, who wrote a little note: "Marlene, clearly no one is on to your theory. . . . No one can figure out what's going on, so your book on 'cool' is clearly much needed."

It is significant that the *Wall Street Journal* considers this front-page news, and I don't believe it's that white America is happy to hear these statistics. If anything, it represents a crisis both in the country and in the business community, where they want and need to incorporate Black people—a major consumer in this country—without alienating the Black male.

It would be fascinating to hear the internal voices of a young Black man reading this headline and a young or older white male reading it. There would be a lot to learn there. This article attests to corporate America's failure to recognize the significant internal struggle Black men suffer with crossing over—and the resulting backlash America dished out during the conservative eighties that caused him to say "fuck it" and abandon the corporate dream.

One of the most successful corporate Black "American" men I know—successful in that he came into this world with little having grown up in the South Bronx and having lost most of his family to alcohol and drugs—was mentored by a Black man in his neighborhood boy's club and was recruited into one of New York's best private schools on an athletic scholarship. He has succeeded in a white company as their general counsel. He now has two kids, is building a new sprawling home in the suburbs, owns quite a bit of real estate (which is where the real money comes from), and has built a vacation home in an enviable location.

I remember him telling me once, a decade ago, that several of the white men in his office were bigots who liked to make racial jokes. My friend said he told himself long ago that these guys would never change, so why should he try to change them? He just ignores them and goes on with his work.

His best friends would find that impossible to do; with the same education, they are employed (successfully, but making much less money) in the inner city. Who is right? Which is maturity? Is my friend's outlook what America would call being a man? Cool says no.

America has *got* to think about this conflict.

Back to the *Wall Street Journal:*

Ellen Scott is a senior human-resources representative at Rockwell International Corp.'s Rocketdyne division. She is young—27 years old—and successful.

Ms. Scott is also part of a fast-growing group in corporate America; Black professional women. Between 1982 and 1992, this group grew a heady 125%. Black female professionals in the 38,000 companies that report to the U.S. Equal Employment Opportunity Commission now number almost 200,000.

This is, of course, minuscule compared with the number of white professionals [*who must be reassured while they read this*]—male and female . . .

Black women are also making strides in the more general category of "white collar, excluding clerical." In 1982, there were slightly more Black women than Black men in that category. By 1992, the number had grown 90% to about 815,000, while the number of men had grown less than 50%, to about 564,000.

Concern for Future

That Black women are rising more rapidly than Black men in corporate America is a source of mixed feelings for Blacks. Considering the obstacles to promotion that minorities of all kinds often face, the success of Black women professionals is reason for pride . . .

Many Blacks fear a future of more struggling, women-led households, fewer men in positions of power and responsibility, and a social and economic disparity that makes the basic social customs of dating and marrying more difficult . . .

The reasons Black women are overtaking Black men are many and complex. They begin with the factors that keep

Black men from entering the corporate world in the first place and include the attitudes that often end up favoring Black women over Black men once they get through the corporate door.

Sidetracked

Many Black men have been sidetracked by crime, drugs and inadequate education; some drop out of the system they are convinced will never treat them fairly. [*This "system" doesn't even know him. The system recognizes a different manhood than what he has achieved. The article now goes on with the usual litany of homicide statistics, jail, lack of college, joblessness, etc. By the time the Black male gets to these ills his cool is in place and well defined. These are the men who got trapped by cool's negative spiral as children. These crime statistics are irrelevant. The* Wall Street Journal *should address the Black men who are prepared and willing to join corporate America. Why are* they *opting out?*]

Attitudes at Work

Armed with diplomas, Black women are getting hired—and working hard to get ahead. In their quest, they are aided, many Blacks say, by both subtle and not-so-subtle attitudes that help them more than Black men.

For instance, there is a feeling among many Blacks, especially males, that Black women succeed because white men prefer working with them. The comfort level has nothing to do with sex [*heaven forbid you should think it does!*], but rather, the theory goes, that ambitious, direct and assertive Black males are often seen by white supervisors as aggressive, suspicious or arrogant. Women are viewed as more compliant, easier to get along with . . .

John J. Higgins, a white senior vice president and general counsel at GM Hughes Electronics and Hughes Aircraft Co., . . . speaks to this issue based on his own experience. He helped mentor Wanda Denson-Low, a young Black woman who is staff vice president for patents and licensing . . . and the company's highest ranking minority female. "In Wanda's case, she accepted me as I was," Mr. Higgins says. "She wasn't looking for an agenda; she wasn't suspicious of my motives. She took me at my word.

"Based upon my interface with Black males, the initial encounters will involve a chip on their shoulder, some obvious skepticism," he adds.

Getting Ahead

But what is perceived by white managers as arrogance sometimes can be the armor Black people wear to protect themselves from the pain of being devalued or misunderstood. Says Michael Sales, a Black senior patent counsel who works with Ms. Denson-Low and Mr. Higgins, "There is a shell; there is a certain defensiveness, a certain distancing thing until the personal relationship develops." He says corporations can help turn around the distressing trend for Black men if top management cares enough to mentor and network with Black males." . . .

Dace Richardson, 34, a project manager with Rocketdyne, sees the white male/Black male relationship as a problem of assimilation. "It's not that you have to act white, you've got to understand the rules to get ahead," he says. "Black men sometimes take a long time to learn that. We want to do it our way. We fail to bond. We focus on being the best engineer, the best person we can be. You need to be competent, but the side that gets you ahead is how well you can work with other people."

Still, most Black women and men interviewed agree that Black men's "maleness" sometimes eventually works for them. Once [white men] realize who you are and what your goals and objectives are and all of the misgivings and misinterpretations have been dealt with, it's a male-to-male exchange," says Mr. Richardson. "From this standpoint, we do come out a little bit better."

So often while writing this book, I have had to defer to the fact that this is a "man thing." What women understand about men is different from what men understand between themselves. And the final rub between Black men and white men is that the Black male's system of manhood might actually prepare him a bit more for the bumps and grinds, the rigors, the unpredictability of corporate life, of street life, of real life. If more Black men had a complete education coupled with cool, they would kick corporate butt beyond belief. Unfortunately, cool stops them from getting in the colleges, getting in the corporations, getting along, and getting ahead.

Southern Cool

I began writing this book in the late 1970s, and actually it is fortunate that I didn't finish it then. But there is one very important interview I conducted in 1979 that offers a lot of insight today.

During the research for this book, I did an informal survey asking Blacks across the country various questions pertaining to cool. I asked many middle-class folks who they considered to be cool, and two names came up most often: Andrew Young and Jesse Jackson. At the time of this survey, Andrew Young had resigned his position as ambassador to the UN and was creating a new political platform for himself. Jesse Jackson was not running for president but was building up a strong national following. It is interesting that these men also happen to be political leaders rather than, say, entertainers, because being considered cool by a large group of people makes you a leader.

I've noticed, though, that when people are asked today who they consider to be cool they tend to name entertainers. Perhaps that's part of a bigger problem in Black America.

It does not necessarily work in the reverse, however. There are many Black leaders that some Black people would not consider cool, for various reasons, among them the fact that it is perceived that whites have made them leaders.

In my survey, Andrew Young was mentioned most often, and without hesitation, by those who were third- and fourth-generation middle and upper-middle class. Jesse Jackson ran a very close second and was named by those who were first- and second-generation middle class. When I contacted Mr. Young, I explained the outcome of my survey, telling him that 95 percent of the people I talked to had offered his name. Mr. Young had an interesting response, one that illustrated the weight and importance cool holds for Black people.

"Flattery will get you everything! If ninety-five percent of your contacts think I'm cool, I am obligated (by my own ego) to respond."

While whites often mistake the term *cool* for *hip*, and therefore relegate it to the function of superficial trendsetting, Blacks at every level see cool as the ultimate compliment.

When discussing symbols of cool, few people will delve into the political ideologies of the leaders they choose beyond the image that their politics conveys.

But since cool is a form of aggression, strength, power, and resilience, a respected political leader might not be considered cool if his political stance is one of nonaggression or nonviolence. An example of this, of course, is Martin Luther King. Dr. King, certainly one of the most important Black leaders of this century, was not thought of as cool, per se; this brings up the notion of mixing cool and religion—oil and water. Dr. King was highly respected, extremely intelligent and articulate, smooth and confident—several of the elements necessary for cool. But it seems that his political stance of nonviolence and his religious faith took him somewhere beyond cool—not to *un*cool but simply to a position outside of cool.

The civil rights movement was based on nonviolence—an important and necessary stance, considering that the movement germinated in the South. But the doctrine of nonviolence came across as submissiveness, weakness, and fear.

I spoke with Andy Young about the disparity of nonviolence

and cool, and through this discussion a definition of southern cool developed:

"Southern Blacks during the civil rights movement and even now," Mr. Young said, "have always had to deal with their situation intellectually rather than emotionally. There is rarely any rioting in the South, and even in the North there are very few cities where an outbreak of rioting has occurred more than once in the span of twenty years.

"Martin was very cool. Cool is ultimately the symbol of strength, a vehicle for self-esteem, a means of survival, and a mechanism for dealing with an irrational situation. Then Martin's cool, and the cool of the civil rights movement, and finally southern cool becomes the process of unifying communities and people, and gaining power through this unification.

"Martin was more powerful than maybe the average person might realize. I sat with Martin and Bernard Lee one night in the Americana Hotel discussing the Vietnam War. He was very worked up about the issue, cussin' and bangin' on tables. And we had all become irritated after hearing it so much. Bernard Lee suddenly said, 'Why tell us? Why don't you tell Lyndon Johnson about it?' I don't know if Martin was serious or not, but he said, 'Get him on the phone.' Normally, when you call the White House they will take your name and return the call sometime the next day. For some reason, here we were fussin' about the Vietnam War at eleven o'clock at night and in three minutes we had Lyndon Johnson on the phone.

"That alone is very cool—that Martin had that kind of power.

"What we were about in the South was transferring power. With all of the enthusiasm and determination of urban movements and overtly violent movements, 125th Street and Seventh Avenue is no different today than it was twenty years ago. Watts didn't change. Neither did Detroit until Coleman Young became mayor and began to rebuild it himself. When I came to Atlanta the Klan ran Atlanta. Now there's a Black police chief, a Black mayor, the superintendent of schools is Black—there was a real transfer of power. Plus the money has begun to integrate. We built the largest airport in the world and Black contractors made a hundred and fifty million dollars on it. We created about twenty new Black millionaires. None of them were rich to begin with. Actually the richest Black man in Atlanta today grew up in one of the poorest neighborhoods.

"No one can deny that power is cool, and cool is power. And the civil rights movement was one of the most successful and most powerful organized efforts by Black people in this country.

"Martin was a very strong and powerful leader, and nonviolence was ultimately the most powerful—and therefore the coolest—of all weapons. There are very few Blacks who have really dealt with power aggressively, and done it intellectually. Do you realize we crippled the entire monetary structure of huge, multimillion-dollar racist cities? We said, 'This city can't move unless we say it can move.' We had five thousand FBI agents following us around constantly. It wasn't easy, but we made real progress."

Mr. Young and I went on to discuss the South and its image in terms of cool. What began to surface was a sense that northern or urban cool is very individual, much more symbolic—things, attitudes, and accomplishments must single a person out as cool. But in the South the individual is not cool, the unified body is."

"During the time of the civil rights movement," Mr. Young

continued, "the baddest niggas in Chicago were the Blackstone Rangers. They had everybody panicked and terrorized. And when we went to Chicago in '66, we decided that if we were going to survive there we would have to work with these kids. And so we started workin' with them. And one of the first things we did was, on the [James] Meredith March we chartered two buses and we took the Rangers to Mississippi. You talk about panicking. . . . I mean, they were *bad* in the ghetto, but in Mississippi they were panicky, and wouldn't leave our side. We had to teach them to deal with the pressures of Mississippi. They were working with a northern cool, and we were working with a southern cool—only we didn't look upon it as a cool, it was simply nonviolence.

"In demonstrations like the one in St. Augustine's we had been literally told that the police were not going to protect us, and there were about four hundred armed Klansmen downtown waiting for us. The police pleaded with us. They said they only had thirty-two policemen and if we went down there we were going to be killed and they couldn't be responsible. It was about nine o'clock at night, and we said we were going to march down there. They were trying to scare us and intimidate us, and we were not going to let that happen.

"We got in a circle and we asked ourselves, do we stop—because that's what they wanted—or do we go on? And I said, 'Anybody who wants to leave is free to leave, but if we turn around now, we're going back into slavery, voluntarily.' And so we just started walking on down there."

But what of Mr. Young and his image? Cool is a very subjective thing; each of us has his or her own concept of what cool is, and therefore a different idea of who is cool. When people named Andy Young as an image of cool they spoke of the way he handles himself—not his politics or his accomplishments, but the style in which he handled his ambassadorship, and his manner in the media. Many feel uncomfortable naming him because he is third- or fourth-generation middle to upper-middle class. Where is his stint with the street?

I mentioned to Mr. Young that Blacks felt very proud of his ambassadorship and of the way he handled his resignation—it is difficult to be cool when you carry an entire race on your shoulders.

"I found that people have to be true to themselves when they get into the political arena. That's what I felt I did," Mr. Young explained.

"When I had my little church in the country, I had to relate to that in the same way. The preacher wasn't supposed to dance, the preacher wasn't supposed to play basketball—the preacher wasn't supposed to do a lot of things. But you have to decide what you're about and then be willing to pay the price.

"I did what I felt needed to be done during my ambassadorship. But I went into it willing to pay the price."

It seems that an understanding of "the price" and preparing himself for paying it is what allows Andrew Young to be cool. He plainly sees strength in the ability to face a situation head-on, to deal with it directly, to recognize the consequences of his actions, and to be true to himself regardless of these consequences. That willingness to put yourself on the line with the confidence that you will be able to back yourself up is the essence of cool.

"Some of the most militant Blacks I know are those intellectual Blacks who work in the upper levels of the white corporations, Mr. Young said. "These are the ones who most want to knock the hell out of white folks. Yet these are the ones who can't riot. These Blacks have very few channels for expressing their anger directly. One of the things that I was taught, and that I *learned*, is not to take it in; to express my anger, my disagreement, my dissatisfaction; myself, to the people directly.

"An incident I'll never forget is one my daddy told me about his father. My grandfather ran a saloon in a little country town in Louisiana. He was also treasurer for several chapters of the Masons. So he had a lot of Black folks' money in the bank. One Sunday the sheriff came in and closed the saloon, while the white folks' saloon was still open. So my grandfather opened his saloon back up. So the sheriff and his men came there and threatened my grandfather if he didn't close down. Well, on Monday morning my grandfather went to the bank to withdraw the money. The money represented the money of almost the entire Black community, and it was the biggest account in the entire state of Louisiana. Well, when they asked him why he was withdrawing the money he said, "You no longer know how to treat Black folks here. I'm gonna move to New Orleans because if I do like everybody else here, my life is in danger.

"They couldn't afford to lose that money, so they got the sheriff to get off his back.

"He dealt with it directly. And through the power of money he gained satisfaction."

I asked Mr. Young who he thought was a symbol of cool, who he would flatter with such a title.

"Arthur Ashe."

His answer fortified the theory that cool is subjective and is dictated by one's peers. Arthur Ashe was a sports figure, and by my own rules he was supposed to be a given as cool. But tennis, back then when I interviewed Mr. Young, wasn't the type of sport normally associated with cool, like basketball, football, and boxing. It was considered a "white" sport, or at least a sport for people with money. And, although Blacks were quite proud of Arthur Ashe because of his success in that sport—especially because it was a white sport—he was not deemed cool.

Because Ashe played a white sport, the masses assumed he lived a privileged life. Mr. Young was quick to point out that he himself had lived a privileged middle-class life, but this was no secret to the masses. Mr. Young's cool was awarded him because of the exposure he'd been given, which allowed the people to see his style, convictions, and basic ability to deal with the political framework of this country.

"Arthur Ashe is so cool it's almost embarrassing," Mr. Young stated. "His tennis teachers knew from the start that he couldn't survive in that world unless he was cool. Ultimately, Arthur Ashe internalized so much of his emotions that it may have contributed to his heart attacks.

"I guess people don't realize that Arthur Ashe did not come from a privileged background. A Black doctor took Ashe and a bunch of other poor children around to the tennis tournaments. There were many other children who could beat Ashe on the court, but the reason the doctor chose to work with Ashe was because he knew he had discipline and a controlled temperament to survive.

"Although this is not an individual, I consider the children in South Africa to be cool. The sixteen- and seventeen-year-olds who are leading demonstrations directly in the face of the South African military are the coolest youngsters I've come across since the earliest days in Mississippi and the civil rights movement. They're very intellectual about it, even to the point of accepting death as inevitable yet determined to go ahead regardless."

Perhaps Mr. Young feels a kinship with these young people because he'd faced the same kind of danger when he walked with Martin Luther King. Perhaps walking with that type of danger—the danger of death itself—and determining to face that danger and emerge not only alive but successful, can give someone the confidence and ease to face any other obstacle without being ruffled. And perhaps that is why so many people consider Andrew Young cool.

Andrew Young ultimately sees cool as something extremely positive for Black people. He put it rather succinctly:

"Cool is a total integration of personality so that you can deal with everything around you. You are in control of your total environment."

So finally middle-class cool is simply another step in the evolution of cool. It is no better, no higher on the scale, no more functional than street cool, which is very much alive and always will be as long as Black people have to deal with the streets. It will probably be a long time before a new strain of cool emerges, because true cool responds to a need. It functions for all of us, adapting to our needs. It is a gauge, a tool, a symbol. And from the highest political figure to the kid on the block, cool is a title to be cherished.

chapter four

Electronic Cool

(popularly known as Commerical Cool)

"My Prerogative."

—Bobby Brown, 1988

I t's the nineties. What's happening with cool today?

We all know the images—knocker earrings, bald heads, buzz cuts, and Nikes (occasionally interchangeable with Reeboks or Cons, *if* they come out with something spectacular). There's something very interesting about these images, though. These styles, or minor variations of them, have been around now for at least ten years.

In the earlier days of street cool, a certain pair of earrings were cool for about a year, maybe two. A hairstyle only lasted a few years, including the Afro, which began to get edged out by cornrows, Jheri curls, and finally straightened hair, again (for all the middle-class cool people in the corporate world).

Styles have to change, and quickly, on the streets of New York, because it identifies your place, your status. It's true that eight-ball jackets became double- and triple-fat goose down coats pretty quick, and that the lingo on the block changed from *def* to *fat* and then to *butter*—all meaning *really nice*—with equal swiftness; and it's still true that boys prove their prowess, or ignorance, by knowing which of those terms to use or which of those jackets to wear. But the overall style—baggy, big, and buzzed—has been around for over a decade.

There are other differences today in cool and how it's demonstrated. Guns and drugs have made the greatest impact on life in the inner city as well as on cool. Frankly, cool almost became obsolete during the eighties because of guns and drugs. Kids today have gone way beyond the definitions and confines of the cool many of today's adults grew up with. Cool on the streets today has become *cold*, and terrifying.

Arsenio—who is he? Is he cool?

Arsenio . . . Skinny, not very attractive, "Gumby" (shows a lot of gums when he smiles or laughs). All these elements should not add up to someone who was considered cool.

Arsenio Hall is the son of a minister. If you've ever spent time growing up in the inner cities of America you know that the kid in your class or on your block whose father was a minister was inherently uncool. And worst of all, he was always the one in class who tried too hard to be cool. The son of the minister had a lot to prove, because his upbringing was so uncool. He grew up with rules, with fatherly discipline and with a direction which was usually very traditional and conservative—in other words, he grew up corny. The rules of the church would often force a young boy to ignore or reject most cool behavior, unless he rebelled and rejected his father (which we see no evidence of from Arsenio's persona) or tried to be cool when he was at

school or around the block, a dangerous proposition. He probably resorted to humor *a lot* to be accepted.

Sinbad—who is he? Is he cool? Son of a minister, inherently
uncool, and always the one in class who tried too hard to be cool.
Hey, this sounds familiar. There seems to be a pattern here.
While violence and poverty prevailed in the real world, plas-
tic and very odd images of cool prevailed on the screen. The
representatives of cool who began appearing during the 1980s
seemed manufactured and handpicked. The eerie phenomenon was that everyone wondered, Who picked them? The
dilemma cool was finding itself in was being played out on
screen during the 1980s. Once again, the reason had its roots on
the streets of America.

The inner city was changing rapidly, while a growing, and
very separate, Black middle class was struggling with a new
identity: mortgages, corporate bosses, and demanding children
who needed braces, a private education, and clothes that iden-
tified them as either cool (if they still lived near the inner city)
or very, very Gap (if they lived in the suburbs). The boys in the
'hood no longer benefited from a diverse neighborhood. The
middle class, in most cases, had fled the inner city or were so
caught up in the demands of making money and staying ahead
that they became disconnected from the problems in the community. The eighties was a time for the high rollers. Everyone
else was ignored, left behind, or taken advantage of.

The children of the sixties, the infamous baby boomers,
were becoming parents to kids who were now the age the
boomers had been when the sixties broke out. These parents,
who were busy trying to keep up, get their heads together,

make money, save the planet, and get in touch with their inner child, were also having to cope with teenagers who seemed to be out of their control. (Not *out of control,* but out of *their* control.) The parents didn't seem to have much respect for the attitudes and style displayed by their youngsters. I believe the reason is that to their parents, America's young people—Black, white, or whatever—seemed to lack conviction, direction, purpose. Parents were smug about young people's attempts at being political, being cool, or being rebellious. Teenagers' rebellion didn't elicit the awe from their parents that their parents rebellion had when they were young.

During the sixties, the hippies, revolutionaries, and dropouts were not going through a phase simply as a matter of course, which is often the way the sixties are depicted today. It's important to remember that from the fifties through the late sixties, young people had witnessed the brutally violent deaths of their collective fathers, mentors, gurus and idols—John Kennedy, Robert Kennedy, Martin Luther King, Malcolm X, the Big Bopper, Ritchie Valens, Jimi Hendrix, Janis Joplin, Jim Morrison, Buddy Holly. John Kennedy was a young and attractive president. He captured the attention of a younger and "different" America and his election was decided on the basis of the first televised debate; once again, television was influencing the country. When Kennedy was killed in front of millions of Americans, adults *and* teenagers lost their direction, their blind innocence, and their sense of omnipotence. Suddenly an entire generation of Americans—regardless of color—were without their leader. This was also the largest generation of young people in America's history.

After this huge generation of young people watched the brutal assassination of their president, they watched in outrage as their government stumbled around and offered flimsy answers to explain his death. Their parents no longer seemed omnipotent, because they too were confused and in shock; they too were without answers. Parents couldn't explain it away or make it all better. Their lack of power, their impotence, became clear to their children in the most public of ways.

So, for perhaps the first time, Americans of all classes were victims of the violence of the streets. American adults lost control of their children. These kids started raising themselves, and raising hell. And, since they no longer revered or even trusted those in authority, including their own parents, they did what children do—they created their own code of maturity and their own style of being. With the escalation of the Vietnam War, parents and children and the government were at war with one another.

Simplistic, admittedly. But it seems as though the foundation for the hippie movement, and consequently the reason traditional American life changed dramatically, was now in place. We can debate forever whether the upheaval of the sixties was positive or negative. But whether good or bad, right or wrong, this exploration and rejection of general society was the first time white people had genuinely experienced something close to what young Black boys had always gone through. *It was the first time in history the country as a whole had experienced cool.*

How can this experience be equated with cool? Because young people were without traditional direction. The father figure—the president—had been taken away. Everything was questioned including God and mainstream religions. This opened the door for Zen, est, Buddhism, and all kinds of spiritual exploration. Being a hippie filled a *need.*

During this search for identity—for leadership, direction, maturity, manhood—young people embraced Timothy Leary, the Beatles, the Maharishi, and Manson. Drugs proliferated, sex was rampant, crazy clothes and long hair were everywhere. Spiritualism and enlightenment were the order of business for the decade. Whites of all class levels became "friends" with Blacks of all class levels. Even in political circles, it became chic to socialize with Black Americans. Eventually, embracing civil rights issues showed compassion and strength.

And through all this the silent majority sat at home feeling that the country was a mess! There was no direction, a war was going on, young people—even those in college—were out of control, the church was losing its stronghold. Good, solid Americans did not understand and could not control their young people.

Sound familiar?

Without a father, boys raise themselves and create a code of manhood that works for them within their environment. That's what the hippies were doing—except that white Americans still had a father in the home who was trying to provide that traditional father image. Simply put, that traditional father image was no longer valid, because that father couldn't make it all better, he couldn't make it go away, and he couldn't explain what the hell had happened. (A similar type of "impotence" can occur when a Black male's father can't make his world better.) This caused a major and perhaps permanent conflict between traditional father and radical son. This sense of impotence, coupled with the women's movement and the economic necessity for white American women to work, eventually coalesced, giving rise to a need for the return of the macho male of the eighties and the white male American's search for his primitive self in the woods of the nineties, courtesy of Robert Bly. The American male was in need of collective therapy.

White America's stint with some of the elements of cool—which, in their case, was based on a rejection of America's standards (rather than simply being a result of isolation from those standards)—was short-lived. The hippies of the sixties turned to drugs and the junior execs of the seventies turned to sex (thanks to birth control pills, abortion rights, and Gay Talese). Everything and everyone was out of the closet—homosexuals, prostitutes, cult leaders, et al.

When the eighties rang in, it was time to grow up. The silent majority was fed up and organized. They might not have been able to explain the Kennedy killing back then, when they were parents of teenagers, but they were wiser and stronger now. They said to their children (who now had children of their own): *It's over and done with. That's that. Life is tough. Get over it. Get your act together. What doesn't kill you will make you stronger.*

Also, America's embittered southerners decided to forgive the Republican Party for having set the captives free back in 1865 (don't forget, Lincoln was a Republican), so they joined up and began voting to fix the party, which had caved in during the civil rights movement (those damn liberal Democrats were responsible for the chaos, because everybody knows that whenever something is wrong with America it's because Black people are getting too uppity).

It was time for a father figure to step in and take charge. Tough love, discipline, family values, the work ethic . . . all these traditional notions had to come back in force. But first, the last vestiges of the sixties had to go, or it might not work. John Lennon's murder heralded the eighties and left behind depressed, confused, and leaderless ex-hippies by the millions. Muhammad Ali, the last remaining Black political icon of the sixties, had been rendered a vegetable by this time. (Call me paranoid, but I still don't believe this mysterious illness he's supposed to have. If you were a young fan of Ali's you might remember the abrupt and confusing change in his personality just before the second Spinks fight. No, that was not the result of too many blows to the head, and it doesn't look like any disease I've seen before. For athletes, who tend to be somewhat apolitical, Ali was as influential as John Lennon. If Ali were as healthy today as Joe Frazier—a man whose entire strategy was to get hit in the head—he might be chatting with David Brinkley on Sunday mornings at least once a month).

The loss of these men had such a profound effect on millions of young people who were now entering full-fledged adulthood that a new father figure, Ronald Reagan (who used to be so comforting when he introduced *Death Valley Days* and 20 Mule Team Borax)—preaching "Mornings in America" and signifying a "new day"—was seen as a breath of fresh air, a leader, a savior.

Money took the place of spiritualism; when your kid can't attend public school and you need money for private school, the grindstone becomes a great place to hang out. And that old institution, racism, was back in vogue. The country was divided like never before, at least not in my lifetime.

The eighties was a decade preoccupied with the very rich and the very poor. *Lifestyle of the Rich and Famous* and *The Cosby Show* were complemented by multiplatinum rap groups. The kid in the middle—neither rich nor poor—was ignored, big time.

What does all this have to do with cool? It's important to understand what America, white America, was going through, because during the eighties and into the nineties, for the first time cool became directly affected by white America. Blacks were no longer outsiders. When McFadden and Whitehead sang "Ain't No Stoppin' Us Now" in the early eighties, it became an anthem for Black America. Black people were in the corporate world and the world of finance; they were teachers, politicians, doctors, lawyers, ambassadors to the United Nations, Supreme Court Judges, and on and on. And they were not just the tokens of yesteryear, nor exclusively members of the traditional Black upper class who had always managed to become professionals; these were Blacks from all walks of life, who were now educated and skilled *and* who were knowledgeable about life in the streets of America.

The deification of greed in America became so prevalent that it was translated and then played out on the streets of America. But the streets had become distinctly different from what they had been.

As a metaphor for what was occurring throughout the nation, I'll use New York's South Bronx during the midsixties, when the Cross Bronx Expressway was being built. This major thoroughfare linked many neighborhoods in the Bronx, making them more accessible and broadening the horizons of those who lived there. More important, though, the Cross Bronx Expressway allowed Interstate 95 to cut through New York, so that traffic flowed from the New Jersey Turnpike through the Bronx and directly into Connecticut, without stopping. While to the rest of the nation New Jersey and Connecticut might seem like separate states, to New Yorkers they are considered suburbs of the city—part of the tristate area, as it is commonly called.

As S. H. Fernando points out in his book *The New Beats: Exploring the Music, Culture, and Attitudes of Hip-Hop*, because of the Cross Bronx big businesses were able to leave the city, and these businesses eventually took their middle-class employees with them. Co-op City was built at the very tip of the Bronx, a major metropolis featuring rows and rows of huge high-rise buildings in which all the apartments are co-ops. Many struggling middle-class families some who once lived in the projects, scrimped and saved and moved into these buildings and into many others like them. This quick retreat to the suburbs, or at least to the outskirts of the city, left the inner city devoid of diversity, of professionals, or of those upwardly mobile people who sought the American dream in traditional ways. Soon neighborhoods such as the South Bronx became wastelands, save for those caught in poverty, and their children.

Black America was now divided. The good intentions of successful Blacks to help others stuck in poverty were laughed at. Many of the inner-city Black kids were hostile and bitter toward the upwardly mobile Black person (or Buppies). While the inner city respected the high rollers—Oprah and the two Michaels, Jackson and Jordan—they were hostile toward those seeking the good life here on the ground. Black kids trapped in the cities didn't go so far as to call the buppies Uncle Toms, because they knew about the revolution and of that generation's commitment to it—they simply had little respect for them, assuming as they did that buppies could no longer relate to their situation.

There began to be a seesaw effect. People seeking the good life felt resentful toward people in the inner city because they felt the inner city's hostility toward them—yet at the same time they themselves felt a kinship with the inner city and wanted to help. But was it help or pity? That was what the inner city's residents wanted to know. Also, those who had "moved on up" as a result of the revolution had become disillusioned themselves. Either their progress had been impeded on reaching the immovable glass ceiling, or they felt the distinct ill effects of the revisited racism of the eighties. And they conveyed this disillusionment to their inner-city brothers and sisters, making them feel less hopeful that hard work and doing the right thing would prove fruitful in the end.

Crack and guns made it easy for the buppies to flee or ignore the inner cities with a clear conscience. Those Blacks with upward mobility who had not lost their cool fought the battles from inside the corporate or political environment, trying to pave the way for a better future. But meanwhile, the community was divided.

The Origins of Rap

It was in the South Bronx that the rap music phenomenon began. One glaring bit of evidence that its roots are in poverty is the fact that many of the records are rerecordings (known as samplings) of hits from the seventies. An MC would make his own mix and create a rhythm and poetic statement that was spoken over the music. Rap was talent and creativity expressing itself in spite of a lack of instruments, studios, or fancy equipment. (This is an important element of the hip-hop generation: The music—especially as it has evolved into gangsta rap—reflects the plight of the children of poverty.) Rap artists made music not with instruments but with their bodies, using sounds to imitate percussion instruments and rhymes to create the beat. Rap music expressed many things, but one thing it demonstrated that should not go unnoticed was that money and space just to create music were not available anymore. Music was created out of what already existed.

MCs who had gigs on preeminent Black radio stations such as WBLS and KISS-FM in New York mixed records better than the original productions. Yet these MCs were not half as talented as those found at house parties, street parties, and clubs. The youth of the inner city was fired up. And soon the battle of the MCs was on.

Reputations were made quickly. Rapping, emceeing, and dancing became a form of competition and a means to make money. Rap evolved into a serious art form, then quickly into a moneymaking venture.

One of the most prolific and respected rap artists is KRS-ONE. Chris Parker had been a victim of the poverty and violence of the streets, he had been in prison, had been homeless. His message was the universal message of young Black men and women trying to make their way in the violence and poverty of a racist society. What is most interesting about his career, though, is that according to *The New Beats*, KRS-ONE was being produced by some unsavory characters whose main source of income was pornography. Creating a record label became a good way to launder money and perhaps to even make some. But crooked business owners are not usually trustworthy when royalties begin to flow in, and Chris was finding himself cheated.

Chris only produced one project with this company, but his entree into the world of business in the inner city bespoke the realities of life in America's streets.

Cool had previously been a method of eventually avoiding violence; once accepted as cool a young man was not challenged every minute of the day. However, beginning in the eighties guns and violence took the place of attitude, style, and simply "proving" oneself. Cool was not being dictated solely by the boys on the block. With the advent of crack and the rise in popularity of rap music, money and the requisite organized crime faction began to prevail in a heretofore unheard-of way in the inner city. It has often been stated that Blacks don't bring drugs or weaponry into the country, that that level of criminality is masterminded by influences outside the community. Is it the mob, big business, independent contractors, the government, or all of the above? I don't know.

I remember a very telling incident on *Mike & Maty*, a perky morning talk show which happened to be on one day as I was typing. James Brown was the guest, to my surprise. Mike asked James Brown, as casually as he could for someone who was completely out of his element, "So, what's going on today with our youth? What's with the violence?" James Brown made it clear that what he knows best is the music industry, and then proceeded to say that the record companies are all financed with drug money. Mike was startled. Did he really say that? Did that just roll out of his mouth so easily? Did this major, revolutionary, incredibly revealing statement just get said on national television by one of America's most successful, respected, and experienced artists, on his little morning show? "What the hell do I do now?" I'm sure he was thinking. What did he do? He misled America into thinking that corruption doesn't exist in our fine major corporations by saying, "Not *all* record companies, right?" Many Americans undoubtedly finished that thought this way, "Just Black ones, right?"

Meanwhile, back at the ranch, conservatives were in power, so while the hippies of yesteryear were trying to figure themselves out, the conservatives were having a party. If you had money you partied big time. If you were a traditional American beauty you were successful. If you had been a member of the ROTC you could be vice president. *Jeopardy!*—formerly considered an egghead game show—was a national pastime.

It was a high old time, just like before the Civil War. The hippies were on the ropes now, trying to make money after they had dropped out of school, had smoked dope, and hadn't prepared for inflation. Liberalism was anathema; examples abounded of how it hadn't worked (depending on how you read the data). If there were people who couldn't get a job the president didn't know why—there were plenty listed in the *New York Times*; *homeless* became a new and accepted word. When the air traffic controllers went on strike they got fired *because workers do not tell business owners what to do*. The Equal Employment Opportunity Commission, which traditionally had turned a sympathetic ear toward job discrimination, was now headed by Clarence Thomas, whose race should have ensured fairness toward other Blacks but whose department didn't seem to respond to racial cases the way it used to in the seventies. White women were working so hard they couldn't get pregnant, and when they did their babies were being raised by child molesters. AIDS made Hollywood and Greenwich Village's Christopher Street subdued and very scared, and removed them from the political arena as any kind of force.

And somehow Black people got the message that it was all their fault. All of it. Everything. From Willie Horton to quotas, taxes for welfare, poor service at the all-Black post offices, drugs, guns, AIDS, Clarence Thomas . . .

Cool Becomes Cold

Cool was now more than ever in a response mode. Rather than cool dictating to its neighborhood, the country was dictating and cool was responding. The president was making it clear that money made you a star, so street-bound Blacks were going to make mo' money, mo' money, mo' money, by any means necessary. The violence and the money were flaunted, as though a child were saying to its parent, *Oh, yeah? I'll show you.* The chant was, if you made money you could live your life your own way. It was your prerogative. The president declared ketchup a vegetable and when reporters asked about the unemployment rate, he pulled out the classified section of the *New York Times* and announced that jobs were obviously available because this section of the paper was "pretty thick." With this eighties fuck-you attitude—directed at America's "deadbeats" (translation: Blacks)—young Black people reacted.

The gentility of the earlier days of street cool was being replaced by an aggressive, desperate method of attaining manhood—that cannot be labeled *cool*, but is best described as *cold*.

This new level of being a man was created through a system of violence, drugs, and mayhem that were much more vicious than they had been in previous decades.

Back when street cool was simply a mechanism for survival—when there was no other choice but the streets—boys challenged other boys, making them prove and thus establish themselves in their 'hood. Beginning in the eighties, street cool lost its innocence and its simple rituals. Now, instead of saying, "Show me what you got," and being ready to throw down, boys were saying to one another, "You ain't got nothing, motherfucker," and blasting.

Because of the greed of the larger society, street society turned to violence for money. The drug on the street was crack. It was cheap and accessible. With cocaine and crack, money changed hands quickly. Big money. With that kind of money, the subtleties of cool were lost. Money and guns were a quick and easy way to prove your manhood. If you showed your money and someone still questioned your cool, you showed your gun; if he still questioned it, you shot him. As in the movie *Grand Canyon*, no gun, no respect. No respect, no manhood.

Cool became more sinister, more visibly angry and outwardly reactive. *Cool*, was no longer *necessary*. Cool did not respond to a need for it. Yes, the doors to the corporations had slammed shut in the eighties, and no, student loans were no longer readily available from the government. But millions of Black teens were in city, community, Black, and some private colleges. Jobs that traditionally had not existed at all for Blacks in the fifties and sixties were now up for grabs. While the opportunities were limited in comparison with those of a decade before, survival was no longer limited to those who were streetwise. Cool was no longer simply a method of survival and a way to obtain manhood, because regardless of how much some political forces would have us believe that there are no avenues out of the inner city besides crime, there are. So the need for traditional cool and its rules for becoming a man were changing, and cool was being threatened with extinction.

Being cool began to be one of two things—either a response to conservative, accusatory America, or a horrible, destructive, frightening method used by young Black males to force other young Black males to chill out and stay put.

The streets were no longer the only choice; therefore, cool did not serve the same urgent need. Being cool—or now, *cold*—and remaining a part of street life became a mandate, and therefore took on a more sinister tone.

Since the eighties are not that far behind us, it is difficult to synthesize all of its ramifications. Needless to say, the idea of the community itself mandating that young Black boys adhere to the rules of street cool—or street life as found in the volatile inner city—is a controversial one. But it is possible that the idea existed and was knowingly perpetuated by some Blacks, and by many whites, who benefited from this mandate.

An example of the feelings the community reflected onto itself was the 1992 movie *Mo' Money*. *Mo' Money* featured Damon Wayans, a Black man who not only came from the projects of New York City, but whose *persona* came distinctly from the projects of New York City. His humor had an edge. He wasn't just funny, he was dangerous. He and Eddie Murphy shared a style which was familiar to many people who grew up in the projects or who knew people who did. They're funny, especially if they're your friend. But their humor can just as easily be mean, cold, biting, dangerous, which is why funny guys sometimes survive the inner city. Their style of humor can be used to protect themselves and to harm others. It is a weapon, a common weapon in the inner city among young men who can't, won't, or don't want to fight. Keenen Ivory Wayans and his television show, *In Living Color,* featured humor that had clearly evolved from inner-city experiences.

The urban voice had been captured and broadcast on television. Now, Mr. Wayans was starring in a movie in which he plays a young man, Johnny, whose policeman father has been killed while saving his partner (who was white, but that's irrelevant). Presumably because of a lack of motivation after the loss of his father, Johnny has dropped out of school and is living a life of petty crime and general immaturity, a life he is teaching to his younger brother. He always dresses in T-shirts, baggy pants, and boots, and when he isn't running a scam, he's shooting baskets.

While selling children's books on the street he meets an attractive Black woman, Amber (who is light-skinned with straight hair—but I'm sure that's irrelevant also), and follows her into the monolithic building where she works. She has an important corporate job. Johnny is inspired to find a job there. Either because of a total lack of skills or because he's too cool to care about the job since he's just there to win her, Johnny gets a job in the mailroom.

To make a long story short, Amber has a boyfriend who also works at her company. He's Black, but barely. He speaks too properly to be real, and he hates everything Black. He's almost nonsexual, a computer whiz who listens to only classical music. He refers to Johnny as "street trash," and implies that Amber could never seriously consider Johnny as her man because he doesn't have the money to buy her. He has tickets to the opera and tells her that the things she wants to do "have no culture." He tells Amber, "Open up your mind to more than rap music."

Tom (yes, that's his name) sends terror through the very fiber of any inner-city Black male watching the film, which seems to say that if that inner-city boy chooses education, a nine-to-five job, and the trappings that America says prove him a success (a *man*), he will end up like Tom. He will need to buy a woman—because he can't turn her on—and he will eventually lose his soul. (Tom strikes fear and loathing in good-looking Black girls as well when he implies they can all be bought.)

Tom is a pretty predictable character. What's surprising is Johnny. Johnny is a "brother." He's sexual, clever, confident, virile, determined, *and* cute. He is culturally correct, and therefore it's implied he is the right choice. Johnny can just look at Amber and immediately tell she once lived in the projects. Very quickly Amber gives up Tom for Johnny and starts dressing in more casual clothes. She's more herself, more comfortable, probably even better at her job (perhaps because sex is better as well? the implication is there).

Given these two choices, Johnny is certainly the more desirable. The problem is, the choices in real life are not that extreme, and for a Black man to aspire to achieve in the traditional American way in this day and age is not as debilitating to his manhood, his Blackness, his *cool*, as these images would have you believe. Success in a chosen career is no longer synonymous with Uncle Tomism or impotency.

But there are still enough Black men who are so threatened by the notion of America's acceptance and what that acceptance will do to them that they perpetuate an image that does not allow younger Black men that choice.

During the eighties integration was anathema—to both Blacks and whites. *The Cosby Show* promoted Black colleges; Kwanzaa and afrocentrism became popular. There was a definite class distinction between those who paid attention to Cosby and afrocentricity and those who did not care about them—Cos and afrocentricity defined being cool for the more upper-class Black kids, while "getting paid," succeeding only for the money, was for those stuck in poverty. Getting along (as in "integration") was not on the agenda and was not cool at all.

The civil rights and Black Power movements had been about creating more opportunities and choices for Black Americans. Freedom *is* choice. But white America, and in response Black America's youth, particularly males, seemed to want no part of the dreams of yesterday, and instead reacted with anger and attitude.

Without the emotional, racial, or political support to choose to leave the inner city, young Black males were forced to carve out a life there.

A young man on the *Les Brown Show* television program (aired December 7, 1993, in New York) explained the choices a boy has in order to get his *props* ("propers," or respect; we have Aretha to thank for this bit of slang). You can either be liked or be feared. In order to be liked you have to dress nice and make others laugh or be fun to be around. To be feared you carry a gun. Period. End of sentence. This young man chose to dress nice, so he stole from Macy's and Bloomingdale's. He did time in jail, and then he had to get his props in jail. Clearly, getting your props is an archaic and vicious cycle.

These choices are a direct reflection of what has prevailed in the outer society. But we cannot blame, totally, white America—black adults have contributed. Many Black adults were the beneficiaries of their parents' ability to "keep their eyes on the prize." They went to college and sometimes succeeded in their chosen career. Yet there were many who still couldn't afford the American dream. Instead of recognizing that the struggle continues, and going on to fight, they became disgruntled and eventually disillusioned. They in turn conveyed to the younger generation—unintentionally—that America is full of it. *Look at me, I did all this and I still don't have much.* Today's adults enjoyed a childhood filled with optimism and faith—Martin Luther King, Stokely Carmichael, Julian Bond, Andrew Young, even Malcolm X managed to convey that America was about opportunity (as James Brown sang, "I don't want nobody to give me nothin', open up the door and I'll get it myself"). These leaders conveyed that America could be forced to do the right thing. The older generation believed that, and their collective positive thinking opened a lot of doors. Their children, the kids who went to college and grad school, came out expecting to reach the absolute top, and when that didn't happen immediately a feeling of pessimism and disenfranchisement took over.

Is this the whole reason, or even the main reason, that such despair and violence exists in the inner city? No. But did a prevailing feeling of disappointment, defeat, and fatalism contribute to the fuck-it attitude of young people in the inner city? Of course.

When young people have a fuck-it attitude, opportunism will

soon take over, and those are the people who prevailed from the inner city: strong, determined opportunists, and few others.

Also, we must not ignore the influence of prison. Many young boys of the inner city had fathers, older brothers, good friends, cousins who were incarcerated. The level of confusion and conflict a young boy must feel when his own father is imprisoned has to be amazing.

Nelson George addressed some of this and more in the "Backtalk" column of *Essence* magazine in November 1993.

Last Thanksgiving I had the extreme good fortune of dining at a party where the estimable author Toni Morrison was a guest. At the same party I also had the extreme misfortune of sharing turkey with a recent Ivy League graduate posing as a B-boy, who spent most of the evening rubbing his designer dreads, name-dropping rappers he'd encountered and mumbling in a slangy drawl worthy of Bell Biv Devoe.

Despite his high-priced education, this doctor's son postured about the room like an exile from *Yo'MTV Raps* trapped in a Harveys Bristol Cream billboard. While Ms. Morrison spoke eloquently about the changes Clinton might make, the pseudo B-boy mumbled about how corny the gathering was. Then, to my horror, he sat down next to Ms. Morrison!

"Why you got to have a brother fucking a cow?" he asked. This was his "critical" response to a couple of passages of *Beloved*. The great writer's face sure suggested disbelief at his crude question. Later a relative told me he'd adopted this street persona in college as his protest against white society and middle-class morality. Oh. I thought he was just an idiot.

While this upper-class clown is an extreme case, his behavior does raise an important issue: How do we make non-street style cool for young brothers and sisters? We associate current street stylings with hip-hop, but in the past, blues, bebop and soul have been our reference points. The problem is that a lot of New Jacks don't see alternative approaches to manhood as empowering.

In the nineties we're confronted with a ghettocentric mentality that thinks speaking proper English is "acting White," that academic achievement is "learning the White man's lesson," and that Blackness is synonymous with lewdness. Part of it is rebellion against mainstream norms of behavior that are perceived as emasculating. Part of it is a lack of class in the current culture that probably has dapper Duke Ellington turning over in his tuxedo.

Preaching alone will not turn the tide. The limitations of this attitude must be held up to ridicule. It must be made "unhip" to be inarticulate. We as a community of creative people must work to make intellectual curiosity, not ghetto dogma, the African-American cutting edge. And this movement won't be as easy as crushing a bunch of rap records with a truck.

Against the potency of street knowledge, a mix of old and new icons must be raised. Right now too few men with a personal style that suggests grace under pressure and whose elegance arose from a cultivation of knowledge are in the spotlight. We need young Sidney Poitiers and Julian Bonds. Wynton and Branford Marsalis, in different ways, have tried valiantly to fit the bill. Filmmakers Spike Lee and Reginald

Hudlin probably come closer to this aesthetic, since both are aggressive, poised and committed to nonghettocentric visions of African-Americans. The groups of Black professionals around the country that are mentoring young teens are doing exactly the right thing. We must begin to celebrate men with brains over brawn whenever possible.

Women can play a key role in deglamorizing street style. Every time a drug dealer, with his Jeep, beeper and gold, gets the best-looking girl in high school a message is sent. Every time *New Jack City*'s villain Nino Brown is called sexy or young women embrace "the gangsta bitch" persona, a message is sent that materialism is attractive, that crime pays and that nastiness has its rewards. Ladies, granting bad boys sexual favors and "dissing" bookworms is a questionable judgment call in terms of values.

Compare the Phoenix Suns' Charles Barkley and Kevin Johnson, for example. Because Barkley has embraced the wild side of his nature he's gotten TV ads and international notoriety. He's a b-a-a-a-d brother. Yes, he deserves his props. But we in the Black community should be paying equal attention to Johnson. Aside from having mad B-ball skills, Johnson may be the NBA's only point guard who reads Hegel and Freud for fun. Now that's flavor in my book.

Reprinted by permission of the author.

Nelson's comments bring up an important element about being cool that is perhaps its most dangerous element. *Street Cool demands loyalty.* The best example of this was demonstrated on a recent *Donahue* featuring Reginald Denny and Henry K. Watson, the man convicted of misdemeanor assault and felony assault in the beating of Denny during the Los Angeles riots.

The audience was angry and hateful toward Mr. Watson. While Mr. Denny was espousing the virtues of forgiveness, acceptance, and understanding of the racial climate that caused everything to happen, the audience, mostly white, was not satisfied. Throughout the show they asked Mr. Watson if he was sorry, and he said he was sorry for Mr. Denny's injuries. No, not enough. They wanted to know if he was *sorry*. Yes, he repeated. Finally, very near the end of the show they called for Mr. Watson to openly apologize to Mr. Denny. He turned and, with a modicum of sincerity but rather deadpan, told Mr. Denny he was sorry for what happened to him and for his injuries. He then turned back to the audience. Something was missing. It wasn't satisfying, not strong enough somehow. After a pause he looked at the audience and shouted, "There, are you satisfied now?"

Needless to say, they were not. He had ruined it completely. And he had ruined it deliberately. But why? He knew that his attitude would null and void the apology. He did it because he has to return to his 'hood. If he lived in suburbia, where his remorse would be accepted and embraced, it would be okay to apologize. But he has to return to the 'hood, where "soft" is vulnerable, where repentance toward white people for something perceived as a highly justified act is anathema, and where doing what white people tell you to do on nationwide television makes you a punk. He runs the risk of no longer being cool, or, since cool really doesn't exist in these neighborhoods much anymore, of no longer being safe. He lives by a different code of what it means to be a man. It doesn't mean *be big enough to admit you're sorry*, it means *be big enough to never have to apologize to anybody*.

The inner city was no longer very diverse in the eighties. It was economically starved and offered few choices to young people in regard to their future. With greed and racism the prevailing American attitudes, inner-city residents felt isolated, picked on, angry, and, most important, defiant. They took matters into their own hands. Many of the boys who chose the life of the streets did so because they were not going to benefit from any of the opportunities created by the Movement. They were children of poverty, uneducated and without a solid family structure. To them, crime and violence were noble paths—oftentimes to them their only path.

A friend, who is a Princeton graduate and a pediatrician, told me this story about her nephew. This smart, attractive, fairly well-educated teenage boy still lived in the inner city. So, of course, instead of getting a job he was lured into selling drugs on the corner. He was being arrested regularly. With each arrest the police would rough him up a bit more. After the third arrest, his mouth was puffy and his face bruised, and his family gathered together to talk to him. "Larry, when are you going to stop?" they asked him. "Look, leave me alone" was always his reply. Finally, in frustration his aunt, the doctor, said to him, "Okay, let's look at it this way. This is your job. You've chosen selling drugs as your career. You've been doing this work for only three months. You've been arrested three times, and you've gotten the crap knocked out of you. You're not very good at this job! You don't have the right skills for it. It's time to retype the resume and get a new job!" This kid is now working for the city, is married, and has started a family.

These "New Jacks" created a highly visible, flamboyant world within the ghetto, accessorized with gold chains, women, expensive cars, and loud music. They were organized, they were successful, they were happy. And, they recruited.

Dwayne Perry is twenty-five years old. He has been a drug dealer and user and has done time in jail. When he was eight he was a good-looking, frenetically bright little boy. With the exception of his mother, who is divorced from his father, his whole family, members of the struggling lower-middle class, all lived in the same Harlem building—his grandmother, his father, his aunts, cousins, and his sisters. By the time Dwayne was sixteen he had been in jail. By twenty he had been to Narcotics Anonymous. By twenty-five, after he had finished his second term in jail for possession, he had stopped selling and was finally drug-free. He now has a son and has moved his little family to Queens.

He returned to the old building to gather with his family after the death of his cousin.

"I hate being around this neighborhood, man," he shouted to his family. "Man, the minute I step out it's about rock and roll. Man, I'll step out and, boom, they grab me up, man. I hate it, man. I'll walk outta here with this on," he said, pointing to his clothes, "and then you'll see me three days later and I'll still have this on. I ain't been doin' nothin', ain't been makin' no money. Ain't seen nobody worth bein' around. But I'll be gone for three fuckin' days. Won't shave, won't wash. I'll be strung out again, and I might even be sellin'," he declared. "I hate it around here. I remember when Nicky was out," he went on, referring to the infamous Black drug kingpin Nicky Barnes. "Things had class. Everybody was cool. You sold, you got paid, you went home to your family. You respected everybody's shit. If somebody had, you knew it was his. You respected that. Today, man. If you in somebody's place and he got five grand, boom, it's yours. You take it, man. That's it, man. Nobody cares about nobody's shit. Five grand, boom, you know it's there, you just wait and you climb in the window, man. If someone's there, you might have to blow 'em away. Man, there's no respect anymore, no class."

This is *not* cool. There is no subtlety here, no respect, no symbolism. This is not about teaching manhood or maturity. This is about money, pure and simple. The splits between the haves and the have-nots was so great during the eighties that it left a society of have-nots who were isolated and therefore created a system of their own, a system way beyond cool. Cool was something all young men wanted to be; Dwayne wanted no part of it.

Recently the *Today* show featured a discussion with gang members in Central Los Angeles. It became clear that gangs represented a sort of caring and protective family to disenfranchised young boys. When asked what the country could do to get rid of the gangs—hire more police, enact more laws, longer jail time—the young men were all in agreement with the gang member who said:

"None of that will work; they've tried all that and it just made us madder. Boys don't join gangs because they want to. But when they're real young and scared [afraid of gangs, most likely], gang members come to them and talk to them. They ask 'em, 'How do you feel? What do you need to get through the day?' Gangs fill a need. Kids just want to be heard, cared about, and feel taken care of."

Gangs have created a system in which they foster a climate of fear, then offer protection to young boys from that climate by making them a part of it.

Things That Make You
Go Hmmm

Television's influence on America's young people was becoming universal in the eighties. For the first time, the electronic media had caught up with the real images of cool in the 'hood (in many cases because Blacks were behind the camera, on the staff, and acting in the film). The occasional accuracy of the media in portraying Black life made the media incredibly powerful as an influence in the Black community. Images of Blacks could no longer be ignored simply because of their inaccuracies. Now television and movies, and certainly the music industry, were portraying "realistic" Black people.

Music videos burst onto the scene and into the homes of millions of Americans in 1980. MTV was a new phenomenon that featured mostly new wave, heavy metal, and experimental music. Sure the station played the same videos over and over again, but it was gaining in popularity nonetheless. Once the original owners sold out to a major corporation MTV went commercial, featuring videos of Madonna, the Cars, Robert Palmer, and many of the other popular groups of the time. Yet despite the popularity of Black performers, Black videos were not being played. After much protesting MTV began to feature the then universally palatable Michael Jackson, and with further prodding it branched out into popular Black music and began playing Run-DMC, Bobby Brown, and Kool Moe Dee. Now, suddenly, teenage popular culture was on the screen. Perhaps for the first time in America's history, street culture was being accurately depicted.

This was a double-edged sword, though. While the Black community's awareness of itself forced there to be more opportunities for Blacks in advertising, broadcast news, television, newspapers, and so on, the flip side was that now the Black community could be captured and guided through the media in the way the white community had always been manipulated. Products could be sold, images created, and minds swayed.

Previously, advertisers had counted on reaching the Black community through their white ads, because if that's the only kind of ad there is, Black people will buy the product simply because it appeals to them, regardless of the color of the actors. Now, that all changed. Black people became more aware of themselves as significant consumers. Jesse Jackson, Malcolm X, Tony Brown, and many others made masses of Black people aware of their economic clout. Their dollars had power. Boycotts and "Buy Black" campaigns made Black folks more selective.

Black consumers have always been loyal consumers. Major manufacturers know this all too well. Loyalty is given either because a company's product works the best *or* because that company used Black people first. An entire generation (my parents') is loyal to the Dodgers because they hired Jackie Robinson back when the team was the Brooklyn Dodgers. Also, thanks to those Blacks who were now behind the camera and who had experienced street life, street culture was becoming an important market. Now, popular culture could tap into the Black market in a more accurate and targeted way. Advertisers played a major part in the bastardization of cool. Reebok, Nike, Converse, and the like began to realize that their product was essential to being cool.

While there were more Black folks behind the scenes in advertising, there were also white-folks-who-grew-up-knowing-Blacks behind the scenes in executive positions in advertising. Before the eighties, images of Black athletes did not sell products very well, or so it was claimed; when someone Black won the gold at the Olympics, endorsements did not exactly roll in. It was a big deal when Walter Payton of the Chicago Bears was selected for the Wheaties box and when O. J. Simpson ran through an airport for Hertz (by the way, I can remember my friends and me remarking that Mr. Simpson shouldn't have to run for anything anymore). By the eighties advertisers were finding that successful Black athletes with a certain style and attitude sold certain products incredibly well. Enter Michael Jordan.

"Money, It's Gotta Be the Shoes."
(Spike Lee to Michael Jordan for Nike)

There is little that needs to be said about the impact of Jordan on the advertising world. But when a commercial can actually have a jingle that says, "I wanna be like Mike," the game is over. This integration brought with it the distillation of cool and its total commercialization. Young white America began to adopt the symbols of cool, and thereby obscured its authenticity even further.

Style was no longer original or unique; it became uniform and very expensive. Style no longer individualized people; it became a definitive symbol of an entire generation. Thanks to all manner of electronic media coupled with capitalism, the hip-hop generation was defined with buzz cuts, goose downs, and attitude. As KRS-ONE informs us on a commercial for Hot 97 FM here in New York City, in order to prevail on the streets of the inner city today one must have a "criminal mentality." Out of a new need, it was cool to be cold. That new need was the need to "get paid," and getting paid was demonstrated by wearing the baddest sneakers, gold jewelry, and down jackets. Also, one gets the feeling that the younger generation was fed up with trying to get it from the white man. The generation before them dressed in monkey suits every day and went downtown, and all they had were bills, bitterness, and hostility from whites.

Bobby Brown heralded in the hip-hop era (even though he was not actually performing hip-hop) in his song "My Prerogative." He ends this hugely popular song by asking why people can't just let him live. Since he made so much money he should be able to finally live his own life. That's what everyone wants. The hip-hop generation made it clear that the only way to get it was with money. Young Black men of the hip-hop generation also made something else clear: when they have enough money to "live their own lives" that lifestyle will be completely their own, and might not be at all similar to America's picture of the good life. Clearly, the message is that if you get paid you can tell everybody "Fuck you."

Young Blacks no longer felt cool in their individuality—they now felt cool as a group, as a generation. The musical groups of the sixties and seventies were named the Temptations, the

Supremes, the Four Tops, Parliament, Blue Magic, the Stylistics, the Emotions, Earth, Wind & Fire, the Impressions, Jr. Walker and the All Stars, James Brown and the Fabulous Flames—each trying to be more dynamic than the last. Today's young people chose names that blended them together and which were almost a code. They sounded like statistics or digits: KRS-ONE, DAS EFX, EPMD. Nicknames prevailed, making the players all the more anonymous to anyone outside this community of young people—Kool Moe Dee, PE (Public Enemy), Flava Flav, Snoop Doggy Dog, Dr. Dre, and on and on.

The interesting thing about cool, or really the loss of cool, in the eighties is that there was a huge group of young people who were almost eclipsed in importance by their parents' generation. The hippie generation had rebelled to such a degree that it almost had a lock on rebelliousness—which is supposed to be the private property of the teenage years. (Is that true, though? Has it always been that teenagers rebel, or was that just a way of explaining the craziness of the sixties?) Black teens had the burden of not only the hippie movement, but the revolution as well. The older generation had done it all.

So cool got lost, as a term and as a basic style of behavior, and many young people had to define themselves—not so much as individuals, which was what cool had previously been about, but as a generation that was cool in its own way, with its own style, its own anger, its own battles to fight, and its own manner of fighting. Since boycotting and protesting was the answer of the previous generation, and didn't seem to have improved conditions very much, this generation adopted an in-your-face, violent style. It was the genesis of *cold*. Have you ever watched a child try to get the attention of a preoccupied parent? He starts off quietly, but before long the kid is screaming and tugging at his parent's shirt. The gun blasts of the eighties and nineties sometimes feel like that to me. *Hey, people, I need your attention! I need help out here.*

Cool—The Thinking Man's Game

Snoop Doggy Dog is one of the most popular rap artists at this writing. One reason why is obvious—he's got a good beat. Another is his cold image—he is lean and stone-faced. He is also misogynistic and self-important. I wonder, though, if Black men were to begin to flex their own muscle and style—with no concern for whites, America, the middle class, the church, the school systems, and the various rules of conduct these institutions attempt to provide—would misogyny and self-importance prevail? So far, they do. On one of Snoop's recordings he raps about how women (bitches) ain't nothing but hoes and tricks. And he speaks incessantly about his "big Black dick." Young girls snap their fingers to songs that tell them to lick on his balls, and to suck his dick. And on *The Arsenio Hall Show* Snoop claimed that he had "one person to thank for my success": his probation officer.

Traditionally, a highly successful recording artist was considered cool because he symbolized a way out of the streets through his talent and determination. Snoop symbolizes how cool has turned cold; his escape from the streets was simply a monetary one. Snoop is still firmly entrenched in the gangsta mentality of the streets.

■   ■   ■

This points out an essential difference between what cool became in the eighties and how it functioned before. Cool can be a vehicle for honest-to-goodness escape, because if a boy follows its rules intelligently he will one day realize that cool itself is a trap and he will let it go. By doing so he will have truly escaped and become a man—a mature, responsible man who answers to himself, not to the community or to his peers, or *for* his race.

This is the ultimate power of cool. So often we see a classroom with lots of white kids and only three Blacks, or a neighborhood where the majority is nonblack; yet the kids are all dressing and acting Black. Why is that? It's because being cool provides self-esteem, pride, confidence, and respect *without money*. In America, where you have very little value as a person if you don't have money, Black boys and young men have developed their own system of manhood and pride and of earning respect through being cool. It is a powerful psychological triumph over America's tunnel vision about self-worth. And that is why it is praiseworthy. Unfortunately, the system for achieving it is so perilous and so emotionally restricting that it is also insidious.

But cool, that vehicle for self-esteem, respect, confidence—manhood—was in danger of becoming extinct. The mind game and subtleties of cool were lost on the teenagers in the inner cities. Guns replaced all that. So, while cold prevailed on the streets, television decided to provide cool. Unfortunately, it also decided that it could now *define* cool. And television decided that cool would look like Arsenio.

For a while the media's Black images—Jesse Jackson, Arsenio Hall, and Al Sharpton—enjoyed a loyal Black audience. They all should've been cool, but they just didn't seem to be *real*.

What was strange about the eighties and cool was that cool was being spoon-fed to the Black community. Either Blacks were being *told* Arsenio was cool, or they were creating their own images of cool as a reaction to the racism and anger they felt coming from the white community. The rappers are a prime example of that. Cool had never been a reaction to America—it was always a system created out of necessity and circumstance. The images of cool on the screen, even though they had come from the community, somehow remained imitations of cool and therefore felt very odd. What was most disturbing, though, was that for the first time an entire generation of young people was faced with white America's direct manipulation of cool through the media, aided by Blacks who wanted to "*get paid*." It became cool to get paid, and therefore cool itself became a product. Cool was about being original, being first, being unique, demonstrating something, being accepted, being strong. The images of cool on the screen had not "earned" that status, and therefore it all felt very odd. Enter Arsenio.

If a Black man could honestly discuss whether he is cool or not (remember, the worst thing a man can do is declare himself cool; while the best that can happen to him is for everyone else to think he's cool), Arsenio Hall might have to admit that he was not the coolest guy in his neighborhood. And he is lucky he wasn't. Those guys are probably still in the neighborhood, following cool's rules.

In the eighties synthesizers dominated. No more need for congas, drums, bass guitars, whatever. Synthetic instruments prevailed—and the music sounded synthetic. Videos—both Black and white—featured fake singers. The Weather Girls—now politically incorrect because of their weight—sang behind the cameras while skinny Black girls mouthed the words on screen.

The battle of the races played out in real life and in every medium as well. If Blacks had Whitney Houston, whites had Mariah Carey (until she informed everyone she was half Black); if Blacks had Michael Jackson, whites had Bruce Springsteen.

Finally there was Arsenio. He cracked us up when he took over for Joan Rivers. In this climate of changing politics, Blacks rallied together and got Arsenio his own show. He earned his place legitimately. But then something happened, something distinctively Eighties-in-America. Arsenio became *what cool is*, and no one seemed to understand the contradiction.

Jason, a twenty-six-year-old, nice-looking Black man from Los Angeles, explained something even more insightful about Arsenio and about the evolution of cool when I asked his opinions: "When Arsenio first made it on the scene I thought he was a big sucka. But over the years the man has gotten strong. I respect a person's growth."

And so, in spite of my biases about the eighties, it has become clear that once again, cool has prevailed. Cool has responded, out of necessity, to money, and it is telling young Black males how to have money—big money—and still be cool. He might not remain cool throughout the process—because the inner city is brutal and it is demanding and it is jealous and scared and relentless and confining, and it will strip you of the title along the way. But the inner city is also very *sure* about what is cool and what isn't, even as cool changes. And, of course, one is not truly cool until he stops being dictated to by cool, and declares *himself* a man.

Recently rap artist Tupac Shakur (who performs as 2 Pac) appeared on Arsenio (a perfect example of someone whose cool is totally in control of his life). He was talking about how the rappers dissed Arsenio, saying *Arsenio ain't down, man, he ain't really wit us.* But 2 Pac had somehow come to understand what Arsenio was dealing with in this American medium called television. And he had come to some revelation that Arsenio was "awright." Perhaps 2 Pac was getting more airtime on Arsenio's show, perhaps behind the scenes Arsenio had explained himself. But the viewer gets the feeling that these rappers that 2 Pac is speaking of began to feel the heat and scrutiny and ambiguity—both America's and the community's—of fame, and came to respect Arsenio as a result.

It is no longer cool to stay confined in poverty. Young Black men of the eighties made it clear to one another that you must "get paid" to be a man—to be cool. Since America closed its corporate and educational doors when it voted in Reagan, and had asked too much of a cultural compromise when the doors were open, cool responded and turned cold. Young Black boys redefined their manhood and found a way to get paid. Most Americans didn't like the choices young Black men of the inner city made for making money, but those choices were limited. Young Black America was no longer interested in tap-dancing on a corner, frying burgers, cleaning toilets, stocking inventory, or opening doors in order to get paid (besides, those things paid very little); not while young urban professionals were sipping champagne out of crystal flutes and dealing in insider trading. They were also not interested in the mental and emotional acrobatics of the cool of yesteryear. Too long, too tedious, too abstract. If they had to be cold to make big money, then cold they would be. And it seemed to pay off—the colder and greedier they were, the more they got paid.

Arsenio might end up showing young Black men how to make big money in America while remaining loyal to the community. He taught Tupac something. Time will tell.

chapter five

Women and Cool

"Hit the road, Jack."

—Ray Charles, 1959

"Ain't too proud to beg."

—The Temptations, 1963

"What a mighty good man."

—Salt-N-Pepa, 1994

"**a**in't Too Proud to Beg" was during the Motown years. When I first decided to use this song title, a few friends told me it was misleading. They said that while the Temps might have been singing this, it was not a reflection of what was really going on between young Black men and women. It was more like these lyrics were giving men *permission* to feel vulnerable, to beg, to let a woman know he wanted her.

I have romantic notions of my youth, but I can't be wrong when I imagine there being a bit more romance back then, more opportunities for tenderness than there are today. Smokey sang about "The Tracks of My Tears" and swooned "Oooh, baby, baby" to his lady. Marvin Gaye, who was considered quite a man, sang, "Ain't no mountain high enough, to keep me from gettin' to you, girl." Teddy Pendergrass told his woman, "Close the door, baby; lay your head next to mine." His voice was deep and gravelly; his beard was thick and dark. He was a man. An adult. The Temps and Marvin Gaye were young, but they were men. Adults.

Today, Black teenaged girls are told, "Wave your hands in the air and shout yeah, I'm a gangsta bitch." The singers are teenagers—young males who seem angry and romantically and sexually immature. The voices of today's singers are also immature and undeveloped.

Something changed, something drastic and damaging. And when you stop and realize that young girls today *are* waving their hands and saying, "I'm a gangsta bitch," it's clear that the change has been broad indeed. It seems to me that the same conditions that created the menace to society lifestyle, created a young woman who is insecure, confused, repressed, desperate, and angry. She needs love and nurturing. Most of all, she needs acknowledgment and support.

A young boy who is fortunate enough to see his father succeed in fulfilling his mother enters relationships as an adult with a rare confidence that he can succeed in fulfilling his partner. He is not terrified of commitment because he knows he can deliver. He also knows that when he doesn't deliver he is still adequate and still deserves love and appreciation for doing his best. He does not condemn himself because he knows he is not perfect and that he is always doing his best and his best is good enough. He is able to apologize for his mistakes because he expects forgiveness, love, and appreciation for doing his best.

He knows that everyone makes mistakes. He saw his father make mistakes and continue to love himself. He witnessed his mother loving and forgiving his father through all his mistakes. He felt her trust and encouragement, even though at times his father had disappointed her.

Many men did not have successful role models while they were growing up. For them staying in love, getting married, and having a family is as difficult as flying a jumbo jet without any training. He may be able to take off, but he is sure to crash. It is difficult to continue flying once you have crashed the plane a few times. Or if you witnessed your father crash. Without a good training manual for relationships, it is easy to understand why many men and women give up on relationships.

Excerpted from Men Are from Mars, Women Are from Venus, *by John Gray, © 1992, HarperCollins Publishers, Inc.*

This description of manhood as it relates to relationships demonstrates the delicate balance between men and women, the arduous journey toward manhood, and the need for a well-edited manual that can guide a man so that he is able to make mistakes and still continue on with his wife and family.

The author believes that the male/female relationship is so difficult and confusing that it might help if we could imagine that men and women were from different planets. If you could you might feel less animosity and resentment toward and have fewer expectations of the opposite sex.

If mainstream America's men and women are experiencing this much trouble with their relationships, one can imagine the confusion in relationships among those who adhere to the rules of cool.

Being cool is about being confident, harnessing anger, maturing in your environment, and ultimately becoming a man. However, at the risk of being politically incorrect (but completely correct about the attitude of the streets), a man is not quite a man without part of his manhood being defined by his relationships with women.

Relationships might not be the right word, since cool does not allow for much "relating." Cool is an attitude and lifestyle young boys "adopt"; few of them are cool by just being themselves. There are rules and codes to cool. As a boy adheres to those rules, the real him might easily get lost.

Talk shows, self-help books, and experts on relationships are always trying to explain that you can't love someone else until you love yourself. In the world of survival, the world of the streets, which dictates that a young boy learn to *be cool* in order to survive, that boy often doesn't even *know* himself.

Women are a constant in the life of cool. Women are both the "keepers of the cool," in that the best woman is the one a young man can trust and let down his cool with, and a means of achieving cool, in that the boy who gets the finest girl is cool. But just like with that leather jacket—is he cool enough to keep her?

The finest girl is not going to stay with a guy who simply knows which jacket to wear. In order to keep her he has to have all the mettle that goes along with wearing that jacket. Actually, it would be a surprise if he was able to snag her in the first place, if he doesn't have the right stuff. She can tell, just as the guys on the block can tell, if he isn't man enough, cool enough, to hold on to his symbols—including her. But he will try to get her because, in this scenario, she is another symbol or possession that takes him farther in his journey toward cool.

Cool is very connected to Black girls. Whenever there is a discussion between men and women about relationships, with the women complaining about how cold men have become because of cool, the men invariably shout, "Well, you like it; that's why we do it." This is true, and it's not true.

As we've already seen, cool is tied to manhood—a manhood that boys define. As with most definitions of manhood—in any culture and in any era in the history of man—cool is about survival, it's about conquering, and it's about achieving success and self-esteem. As man changes, the dangers he must survive are constantly changing as well. Regardless of the nature of those dangers, surviving and succeeding are what make a man a man.

Woman has always sought a man who can survive and conquer. And so, even in this day of civilized and sophisticated society, survivors and conquerors are considered the most desirable, the sexiest. In the inner city, the cool guys are the most sought after.

This is tricky, though, because what is cool? Young women living the life of the inner cities are measuring manhood by the obstacles and goals found in that environment. As discussed in earlier chapters, Black America is diverse; what is cool in one group is not necessarily cool in another. Middle-class cool accommodates those who survive and achieve through education and traditional business acumen; revolutionary cool accommodates a more political personality. There are those in the community who survive because they're funny, so humor can set you apart and help you succeed (although being the funny guy doesn't usually attract the fine girls; he may survive, but he isn't really *cool*). Depending on how a man has achieved his cool, a young woman may find emotional and financial success or become caught up in a dismal, damaging relationship.

In the world of street cool, the coolest guy is often remote and detached. Once a girl gets him, if she is looking for a romantic relationship—not sex, but romance and intimacy—she is either very disappointed or she ends up working like crazy to break down his cool. It will take a great deal of trust before he will ever be able to relax and be himself. The young boy who began the process of becoming a man of the streets is buried deep within layers of cool. The process of unearthing that young man is arduous and often impossible. Seeing who he really is—separate from his cool—requires a great deal of trust, patience, insight, and stamina; a young woman of the same environment might not be equipped with these qualities. And even if she were, she will not be able to do it alone. For a young man to let go of his cool, he needs the support of the entire village. That village is both his immediate community and, ultimately, America itself.

Ghettocentricity—Also Known as "It Ain't Much but It's Home"

On the streets of America, survival does not have the same meaning as it does in the larger society—survival is not the house, picket fence, and recreational vehicle. Back in the old days, the Black communities of America fought for integration. Black people wanted to be judged by the content of their character, and the dream was that white children and Black children would someday walk hand in hand in this great country. However, by the mid-eighties, the doors to better education and financial opportunity that had briefly opened were being slammed shut. The inner-city Black community recognized more and more that no matter how much the Black individual conformed in order to participate in the larger society, the race as a whole would still not be allowed in. The backlash racism in the larger society created a backlash in the Black community that I call, if I may borrow from Nelson George, ghettocentric. Ghettocentricity, as I see it, is about *not conforming, not trying* to fit into American society, *not integrating*. It's about making it and remaining Black—Black as defined by the streets. The problem, though, is that Black as defined by the streets is becoming an increasingly narrow definition and an ever-more-limited lifestyle. In a society where freedom is choice, ghettocentricity can be very confining.

As I sat watching *This Week* on TV one Sunday morning, David Brinkley, Cokie Roberts, Sam Donaldson, and George Will were discussing the mayoral race in Washington, D.C. They were marveling at the fact that Marion Barry had a chance of winning again. Barry—that man we all watched smoking crack in a hotel room with a woman other than his wife while he was mayor—might get reelected? *What's going on?!* Sam Donaldson pointed out that Barry was "using the race issue," but Cokie quickly pointed out that Barry's opponents were Black. Sam, without knowing how astute he was being, said, "That doesn't matter." But, perhaps sensing trouble, David switched the subject. This discussion had the potential of becoming a profound discovery of what is Black today. Ghettocentricity is being played out in D.C. politics. The clash of Blackness is the hidden issue.

Hollywood also has been experiencing a similar clash, but the whites in charge have been ignorant of it, as was Cokie and crew. In a recent article in *Entertainment Weekly* magazine, an interesting scenario unfolded. Trey Ellis, the noted young novelist, presented a sensitive script to Disney, and the movie was subsequently released with the title *The Inkwell*. Having vacationed a few times at Martha's Vineyard, I am familiar with the strip of beach located close to the center of town where the Black summer residents go for their first sighting of old friends. (Get it? A Black gathering spot on the mostly white beach of Martha's Vineyard—the *inkwell*.)

Ellis' script was self-described as "something beautiful, bittersweet, elegant" and he compared it to *Summer of '42*. Disney liked the idea but chose Matty Rich as the director (Ellis was hoping to direct himself). Sure, there were probably many internal business reasons for this choice, but Matty Rich, the then twenty-two-year-old director who won an award at the Sundance Film Festival for his debut film, *Straight Out of Brooklyn*, had a personal background light years away from Ellis's or the people in his script. Rich lived in the Red Hook section of

Brooklyn from ages four through ten, then moved to a neighborhood nearby. *Straight Out of Brooklyn* realistically depicted the grim and hopeless life of a family in the projects in Brooklyn. Ellis, a graduate of Andover and Stanford University, is the author of *Platitudes* and *Home Repairs*.

According to the article, Rich read the script and declared that it wasn't "Black enough." He then began repairing it. Ellis asserted that Rich first tried making the schoolteacher father a garbage man, and had him drinking Colt 45 and cursing. A particularly interesting change was making the Dalmatian in Ellis's script a doll. Ellis was unnerved, noting that the dog and the sixteen-year-old main character were friends; like a lot of kids, the boy had a relationship with his dog.

Ellis fought the good fight for the Black middle class, going so far as to say, "the Black middle class are not very different from white," which is probably why Rich found the script to be not Black enough. The article states:

> Ellis compares Rich's work—the director recently sold a pilot concept called *Red Hook* to Warner Bros. and Fox TV— to "Stepin Fetchit, Black minstrels—making Black entertainment for a white audience. That's the trap young Mr. Rich has fallen into. I tried to explain it to him, but he's got the right thing on one side and a paycheck on the other and he made the wrong choice."

Rich pointed out that, in spite of all this outrage, Ellis had no problem cashing the check for the movie, even though he changed his name in the credits.

Rich became a vocal symbol for the clash between both generations and both classes. Rich commented on Spike Lee, whose *Jungle Fever* was released when his film was released, by saying Lee was a "middle-class third-generation college boy." This managed to offend Lee for some reason, who is quoted as responding, "It's that kind of ignorant thinking that has Black kids failing on purpose in class."

And there's the rub: ghettocentricity, a narrower and narrower definition of what it means to be Black.

Becoming a Man Has Its Rewards.

The male who makes it according to the terms of life in the streets is considered cool, and those males who are cool, who have achieved the highest level of manhood in that environment, get the most girls.

I'd like to observe, though, that America does not recognize the Black woman as a prize or as beautiful, judging by the general depiction of Black women in the media. Strides have been made, but until America loses its narrow view of beauty this will be an ongoing problem. It's easy to conclude that America's insensitivity to the beauty of Black women contributes to a division between the Black and white communities of this country, or at least to a division between Black and white men. If that conclusion were correct, the next leap would be that this insensitivity contributes to some of the problems Black men and women have when it comes to relationships. As a woman, I would think that a man would enjoy seeing his woman (or his race of women) appreciated for their beauty. In order to not be influenced by America's slight, Black men have become more and more removed from and defiant about America.

What is good-looking? What is *fine?*

Why is it that I can find Catherine Deneuve to be beautiful and elegant, but a white person can't see how beautiful Alfre Woodard is. Her complexion, her hair, her full and wonderful lips—it's a different aesthetic, certainly, but beauty is beauty. I am tired of Black people having to adjust to someone else's ideal of beauty; and young Black males are *very* tired of it. The funny thing, though, and another reason why America can be a puzzlement, is that Black women are aware that their beauty is admired. Individually we receive comments, flirtations, or simply appreciation. But those with the power to promote make a conscious decision not to reflect the truth about Black beauty, or of white American's true appreciation of it.

This slight has a big impact on me, but I believe it has an even bigger one on Black men. Mainstream America's ignorance or rejection of the Black female's beauty creates a strange conflict for Black men. She is *fine* to him but not to America. (By the way, he would never admit he even cares what America thinks. He's too cool to acknowledge any hurt. He might be too cool to even know it bothers him.)

Frankly, I can't blame only white America's media for the portrayal of Black women. Black America is also responsible for some unsatisfactory images of the Black female (and Black male, for that matter). Although I grew up enjoying *Soul Train* on TV, there came a point when I simply could no longer watch it. The women on the show seemed to be on display. Their clothes, their attitude—it was all so blatantly sexual. The cameraman loved to point the camera under their skirts. I even know a man who confessed to me that he masturbated while watching the show (a very handsome, successful Black man in his early thirties.) And while the women were sex objects, the men on *Soul Train* seemed like clowns. Their faces were nondescript, their clothes became more and more absurd. The message seemed to be, *Look at the women—these men are no threat to you. They're just there.* There were no men on the show that I could enjoy watching as much as my friend enjoyed watching the women. Yet this was a Black-owned show?

It's a tragedy that so much sex is going on in the inner city—not just because of teenaged pregnancy, but because the Black male could make so much better use of his sexual drive. As with all men, if he were to redirect that sexual drive into his career, hobby, education, or community, he could quickly improve his situation. According to many success-oriented books, the sexual drive (for both men and women) is best served doing anything other than having sex all the time. It is man's most powerful drive, but when it merely is recreational the opportunity to use such a force to propel himself is lost.

Speaking of Sex . . .

A friend of mine who knew I was writing this book came to me to ask my opinion of something she'd just read in a very popular book called *Makes Me Wanna Holler* by Nathan McCall. In the book he describes an incident in which he shoots another boy. He describes it as feeling "better than sex." It's certainly a phrase I've heard before.

I couldn't help feeling very sad. A man who finds shooting someone to be "better than sex" has probably never experienced intimacy or lovemaking. This is certainly not a racial phenomenon, but my concern is with the problems in our community; the rest of America can take care of itself for now. Intimacy is a casualty of life on the edge. Being cool is a Black male's answer to living life on the edge. And so, there is little opportunity for true intimacy. Comparing the feeling one gets from shooting someone with the feeling one gets from sex makes it obvious that sex is being used as primarily a kind of "release." When life is intense, sex does become a release—a release of sexual tension, stress, anger, aggression, anxiety, whatever. But lovemaking, with all its requisite tenderness, trust, caring, and sharing, is much more than a release. And, by the way, is much better than shooting someone, I'm sure. (I must share this thought. I can imagine someone saying to me, *How can you be sure if you've never shot someone you intensely hated?* That is precisely my point: *How can you be sure shooting someone is better than sex, when you've never experienced true lovemaking?*)

Romance Is
a Luxury

Rudy Huxtable is a character on *The Cosby Show*. Her TV family, the Huxtables, are a successful, traditional American family: Cliff and Clair love each other, love their children, and can provide all the amenities for successful child rearing. They will undoubtedly produce successful young men and women. Cliff offers his son *and daughter* a fine model of American manhood. He is cool among his peers and his viewers because although he has Black and white clients, neighbors, and friends, he has not compromised his Blackness and become an Uncle Tom. However, Cliff is not cool by street definitions. Cliff, and Bill Cosby for that matter, has succeeded in a traditional American way—through education, and through family, community, and societal support. He has not succeeded through street cunning and prowess. When I say Cliff is not cool by street definitions, that is not to say he's uncool. He simply exists outside of the need to be defined by the cool established on the streets of America.

Unfortunately, many young boys of the inner cities are not growing up with Cliff Huxtable as their father. Therefore, they define their manhood, their cool, based on their environment. Subsequently, their relationships with girls and women become defined by cool as well, and by the girls and women they encounter in that environment.

Many men have commented that cool would not exist if women didn't like it so much. That's probably unfair. She lives in the inner city as well, and while she may not have to prove her womanhood to other women, she does want to survive the inner-city experience—and maybe one day go from surviving to actually living. So the young Black girl is doing what females have done since the beginning of time: She is attempting to land the male who is the strongest, the smartest, the cleverest, the *coolest*, because he is the one who will ensure their survival—or so she thinks.

Unfortunately, the inner city is not America. It is only a small part of it, and an isolated, almost colonized part at that. Selecting the "coolest" guy might help her survive if she stays in the inner city. But her hopes for that successful "all-American" family will be dashed, as will his, if they venture to or live outside of that environment with only his cool as a survival plan.

The nebulous, intangible rules of cool began with harnessed anger and a need for emotional self-control. It then evolved into style, attitude, and ability to defend oneself. Ultimately, the rules for determining if a boy is cool are established mostly by other boys. The constant concern with and dependency on what other boys think can cause genuine problems for any young woman trying to be involved with a young man from the 'hood. The real catch-22 is that as long as he is concerned with what others boys think, he isn't truly cool, although he might be cool with them. Translation: They won't give him a hard time, but he will not have truly earned their respect.

Minneapolis seemed like a good place to talk to young people about cool. Jimmy Jam and Terry Lewis hail from there, as does Prince. It's in the heart of America, unencumbered by coastlines and the requisite status that comes with them. Yet the NBA All-Star Game was played there, as were the Super Bowl and the 1991 World Series. All this has earned Minneapolis a designation as cool, if cities (besides New York and sometimes L.A.) can be called cool. Although I'm a native New Yorker, I decided not to interview in the coolest city, New York. New York in some ways sets the standard for street cool, but I felt it was important to see if street cool operates in other cities. Needless to say, situations generally tend to be less extreme in Minneapolis, but the young people there had strong feelings about cool.

I spoke to students at two of Minneapolis's "inner-city" schools. Edison High School is a racially mixed school situated in a lower-income neighborhood in the city. It is about 30 percent white, 30 percent Black, and 30 percent Asian, with a few Latino students. A friendly young teacher, David LaDay, introduced me to his class of about twenty students—mostly Black males, with a few Black and Hispanic females.

North High School is a predominately Black high school in a lower-income Black neighborhood that is also in the city. It turned out to be a great place to get a fix on cool.

"He Ain't Cool"

I began both sessions by asking the girls in a general way about cool. "Cool is being yourself, it's getting respect, it's having friends," they said.

I then asked them what they consider cool. Is it the same as what the boys think is cool? The answer to that was No! Unanimously, the girls at North and the girls at Edison showed their discontent. What is cool to the guys is unequivocally not what is cool to girls. This is no small point, because it is the most basic explanation as to why there's problems between Black men and Black women.

Nicole, Brandi, Mia, Kisha, and Lyssa at North talked with me for some time before the boys—Artemus, Gary, Matt, and Brother Tron X—joined the group.

"Girls are about business! They're about being smart, going to school, being a cheerleader, getting a good job, going somewhere in life!" one girl said. (Notice that these are goals America would agree with.)

"The boys are all trying to be cool. Claiming a set (translation: gang). Running the streets," another added.

"My father is 'the King of Cool.' He doesn't smile in any pictures. He's always trying to look hard." This same young lady began talking about her brother. She became more serious, a bit troubled. "I'm worried about my brother. He just goes with the flow. He don't plan for the future. He just smokes weed and cigarettes. He's going nowhere." (Is it a coincidence that his father is "the King of Cool"?)

"The girls who don't care about school are the ones interested in the dealers with the good clothes. I don't want to name any names, but there are girls in this school who are getting straight Ds. They're the ones chasing the boys who are trying so hard to be cool with eighty-dollar jeans on. Cool ain't eighty-dollar jeans, it's thirty-dollar jeans and money in your pocket and a plan for the future."

"This guy," one girl said, referring to a young man who later joined us, "he refuses to take physical therapy for his injury. 'It ain't cool to go to physical therapy,' he says." When he joined us, he concurred.

"The boys I date, it seems like I always have to teach them something. They never plan anything. They don't plan dates to the movies!"

"No, that's not true," another girl said. "They do plan. They plan to sell drugs." No one laughed.

Are those the boys who are considered cool?

"No." Not by them. "But they think they are and those girls think they are."

I then asked the girls, Who is cool?

Several of them named two boys who had already graduated—Malik and Marvis. Why? I asked. "Because they're comfortable with themselves. They kept trying different styles, new hairstyles. They were unique in themselves."

Although I met with them at separate times, I asked the boys at both schools, what is being cool? Both groups of boys agreed—"Being cool is being yourself." Being comfortable with yourself. Getting respect. You don't have to be "all that."

Then I asked, What if a boy wears close-fitted jeans from the Gap—is he cool?

No, nah, nope, no way, Uh-uh.

It was unanimous. At Edison they laughed and pointed at their teacher's Gap pants. At North they just shook their heads in unison.

"So you can't just be yourself and be cool, because if you like your pants a certain style, you won't be accepted," I stated.

One boy at North got honest. "A guy can start off like that, but eventually he'll have to wear baggy jeans."

The boys and the girls have totally contradictory ideas of what makes a boy cool, a man. A boy has to fit in among the other boys to be cool with them. A boy must stand apart and show his uniqueness to be considered cool by these girls.

Many years ago, out of frustration, I asked a young man I was dating why Black men rarely, if ever, hold hands with or hug their girlfriends. Why do you rarely see a young Black man with his arm around his girlfriend while on line at the movies? He thought about that for a minute and then gave me a straight answer (also a rarity, since most of my questions were silly to him; "pussychology," he called them). "Because he can't. He's always got to watch his back."

Vulnerability is a dangerous thing in the 'hood—always has been—and love makes one very vulnerable. A boy of the streets learns that he must get this emotion "in check" because it's too soft, too stupid, and too dangerous. This unwillingness to be vulnerable also contributes to the idea that shooting someone feels better than sex. Again, intimacy and lovemaking require trust and eventual vulnerability.

I remember Robert Townsend, the actor-comedian-producer-director, once talking about how white men were traditionally depicted kissing and making passionate love to their women in movies and even in toothpaste commercials, while Black men were never allowed to be sexual on screen. Obviously, Black men longed for more sexuality and romance in their lives and in their entertainment. So Mr. Townsend, Eddie Murphy, Martin Lawrence, and others have made sure that their characters are sexual. Thus far, their characters *are* more sexual. But more intimate and genuinely romantic? Not yet.

What is romance? The closest examples I've seen from Blacks on television have come courtesy of Bill Cosby. I'll never forget the episodes of *I Spy* featuring Eartha Kitt as a drug-addicted woman he feels compelled to rescue. While it's unclear whether he is smitten or merely sympathetic, Mr. Cosby conveys a compassion rarely seen in a Black man toward a Black woman on screen. And Mr. Cosby later showed lustful romance toward his television wife Clair, to the point where many thought he and Phylicia Rashad were having an affair behind the scenes.

This is not to deify Bill Cosby, but I do want to point out that Mr. Cosby's image, from day one, was never particularly cool as defined by the streets, and so he was free to be his own man.

That freedom has allowed him to show real romantic love for a woman without worrying about what *the boys* will think. (Danny Glover in *Grand Canyon* and Wesley Snipes in *Sugar Hill* also come close to romantic for me; perhaps, significantly, *Sugar Hill* is about a man trying to leave the street environment. And I'm sure there are others I'm just not remembering.)

To get back to my friend, I wasn't satisfied with his response to my question; it felt too much like an easy answer. So I continued to pursue the issue with today's young people.

So, Why Doesn't He Put His Arm Around Her?

I asked this question of the young Black men at North High. The answers ranged from that of one young man who was a member of the Nation of Islam—"Because the Black man has been taught not to find his woman attractive because he is bombarded with the images of the white woman and therefore is not proud of his woman"—to comments similar to my friend's about the Black male always having to watch his back, not being at ease and comfortable enough in the street. I became totally unprofessional when I challenged the first remark, stating that images of Black female beauty have been on screen and in magazines, even if these images were few and were limited to Black audiences, for over twenty years. Since this young man was only about seventeen, I felt that was no excuse. And what about the image of the white man? Black girls have generally stayed loyal to Black males in spite of the bombardment of the white male image. This may sound contradictory to my earlier observation, but it isn't. America must become less myopic about many of its aesthetic values in order to support all its citizens and make this a stronger country. But when a young Black male today won't put his arm around his girl, I am resistant to turn to the white man as the cause.

Finally the teacher, a twenty-eight-year-old Black man, chimed in and said, "When I was younger, I didn't touch my girlfriend affectionately in public because there might be other women in the area I might want to date. I was keeping my options open."

This opened up a discussion of whether Black males are so much in demand that they no longer have to chase, that instead are chased—and, if so, what that does to their relationships.

One young lady confessed to now dating someone white. She was the first to introduce the fact that young Black women do not consider dating outside the race. Needless to say, this created some dissension among those in the group (however, less than I thought it would). It was important to pursue this because a common complaint among Black girls is that they find themselves chasing the boys and they rarely have the thrill of being chased. The boys agreed that they rarely chase because there's so many girls to chose from and because the girls come after them.

I asked if the boys get a thrill when they finally go out with a girl who chased him. A quiet, good-looking young man sitting next to me in the corner said, "Nah. Not really."

Black girls are at the mercy of Black males today because those boys who show promise—either because they're on the right all-American track or because they are supercool (depending on the girl's taste and goals)—are much in demand. Girls are also at their mercy because it's politically incorrect to consider going outside the race. So, with girls chasing them, the average Black boy has become complacent about the average Black girl, and his ego may be disproportionate to his accomplishments.

Although young Black men do have a capacity for love and positive emotions, being cool seriously gets in the way. This is why a young Black girl learns how to be cool herself, which unfortunately ends up with her being defined as a woman who needs little emotionally "because she's so secure."

The most desirable Black girls are the ones who have self-confidence and emotional reserve. However, in many cases this self-confidence and reserve are a veneer, in the same way cool is for many young men. When that veneer is lifted, these girls are no longer desired to the same degree. A girl's "coolness" is the result of surviving the same inner-city experience as the boy has, with some special problems thrown in that all women eventually endure—sexual advances, petty jealousies, competitiveness, the threat of being perceived as promiscuous, or snotty . . . the list goes on and on. As my sister said to me, "Being attractive in the life of the streets is a whole other animal."

Being attractive is certainly a plus, but it doesn't always work in a girl's favor. It is the rare young woman who is able to find that delicate balance between staying confident and not becoming conceited. Most attractive girls don't master this tenuous balancing act.

For the one who does, she is given the respect of being called "fine" and is sought after by boys who are trying to be cool and would love to have *her* on his arm.

■   ■   ■

Why does the Black female have to be all these things? It's simple. If *he* is cool, *she* has to be, or must at least be perceived as strong enough, wise enough, and confident enough to "deal" with him. Can she *deal* with his lifestyle? Can she *deal* with his friends? Can she *deal* with the unpredictability of his life? Can she *deal* with *his* American dream? Can she *deal* with his anger? Can she *deal* with the competition (others will be interested in him)? And finally and most important, can she *deal* with his emotional distance—his cool? Does she need much emotionally? If she does, she's not quite cool enough.

The girl who learns to become emotionally cold thinks she needs very little by way of intimacy. But I believe she does need closeness and intimacy; and she needs it more than the boy who has invested his manhood in cool. He is repelled and threatened by intimacy and vulnerability; *she* simply isn't used to it.

There are many women of the inner city who become emotionally cold themselves, for the same reasons a young man does. The process toward that emotional coolness is the same—controlling anger and emotions, learning to protect yourself, being tough and strong, having an individual style and the confidence to demonstrate it—but the experiences are different. Because a woman can lose her cool and still remain a woman by virtue of nature, she is somewhat exempt from the demands of cool. She does not *need* to be cool in order to have the respect of being a woman.

Often the young women who are good-looking and emotionally cold have an air or attitude that is perceived by others as one of superiority. If that is the case, not only will she be disliked by other young girls, but her boyfriend might challenge her if he believes her attitude is getting out of hand.

"She Thinks She's Cute"

In the inner city, there's no such thing as "thinking you're cute" and getting away with it. It's the same as "thinking you're cool," which is anathema and gets you challenged and quickly taken down a notch. One reason why a guy who is not cool enough can't be with a woman who is truly fine and knows it is that when a woman clearly thinks she's cute, she can cause such a commotion that he may have to defend her and himself. Again, as with the leather jacket, is he cool enough to keep her?

Young women like Janet Jackson and Whitney Houston are not the products of the block. In order for a Black girl to grow up with that level of confidence, beauty, and attitude, there must be a great deal of "protection" (this is not just "protection" against rape and violence, but protection against animosity, jealousy, challenges, and the dictates of her peers, friends, and enemies). For a woman to be as free as these two women—free to be confident in her beauty and sexuality—she must be surrounded by people, particularly men, who allow her that freedom by protecting her from those who would try to contain it. Contrast Janet and Whitney's experiences with that of the actress Dorothy Dandridge—a beautiful but tragic lady who had an attitude of confidence and was put in her place for it. Janet and Whitney demonstrate the potential for confidence in their beauty for all Black women, if only they could afford peace, quiet, and protection.

Keepers of the Cool

The best women become "keepers of the cool." They are the ones who, if they are lucky enough, mature enough, and trustworthy enough, get to see her man let his cool down and be himself (after quite a long time). The best men are the ones who know how to be cool in the streets and who realize that there is no greater freedom than being able to come home and be your true self. A woman who can allow her man to be himself without being afraid that he isn't strong enough, cool enough, or fearless enough is a gem indeed. He should learn to recognize that woman, reward her, and covet that relationship, because there is no amount of "gettin paid" that can buy that level of freedom and happiness.

Let's face it—being cool, all the time, is draining. For the young man who is *truly* cool it isn't as draining, but he might ultimately be so emotionless that he is a lost cause. "Losing your cool" on the block can be damning. If you lose it by being too hotheaded, fighting too quickly, fighting too wild, or fighting for no good reason, all is lost and you may have to fight to rebuild it.

So for the millions of young men who are trying to be cool, where does all the emotion and anger go?

She usually sees a great deal of it. It almost seems as though the unwritten code is that she is the man's release valve. Releasing anger and emotions can manifest itself as yelling, fussing, playing ball, fighting, sexing, drinking. Some of these activities are expected of the man growing up in the inner city, and the young woman involved with him takes the brunt of a lot of his frustration.

This release can have positive benefits (in his view). It relieves his internal demons, and it trains her at the same time. The Black woman of the inner city is not a docile creature, because she too is surviving a difficult situation, *backwards and in high heels*. So she often requires a lot of grooming—if he is willing to put up the struggle. His rage and craziness may eventually wear her down until she's the kind of girl he can stay with. When she becomes this kind of woman—needing very little emotionally, financially, or socially (by America's standards)—he can continue to practice being cool and remaining a child, following the rules that have been set up by children.

It is the fortunate young man who finds a young woman who'll go through all this with him. The most promising possibility is that he will begin to care more for her than he does for his buddies on the street. In the absence of an important older and more mature male directing his goals, *she* might be the key to his imagining surviving more than just the streets. If they can leave the streets, or remain in the inner city and *live* rather than *survive day to day*, he can slowly become more himself—whoever that is. Unfortunately, too many young males have lost themselves altogether and have become nothing more than rigid, emotionally reserved men. As Wynton Marsalis pointed out on a recent *60 Minutes*, a hipster is a guy who witnesses a car crash and just sort of raises his eyebrows. That takes a lot of training. The irony is that being himself is *what is cool*, but most young men are trying so hard to be cool they miss the whole point. Together he and she can set goals and plans, and he might begin to want those goals more than the goal of gaining the respect of his street friends (which never really remains constant). But that woman must be mature, and her goals must be well balanced, not unrealistic.

He is very hesitant about ever letting her see who he really is, because she will then have a great deal of power over him. Too often, young women betray that trust and blow their man's cool by talking about him to others, laughing at him, rejecting his admission, and breaking that tenuous bond he's been trying to develop. If he loses that sense of trust because of her betrayal, he may never regain it. That's when girls can become "bitches." Quite often young women betray men's trust out of fear; they simply don't know how to react to this new side of someone they may have known for some time.

Bitches and Hoes

A friend of mine is divorced and raising two young sons, now aged ten and twelve. To help her through their puberty years, she thought it might be a good idea to buy an issue of *EM* (*Ebony Man*), a magazine for young Black men (teenagers). An article appeared in the magazine she bought, and she and I stared at it in dismay. Things have changed a lot for young Black women since we were young. The art of flirting, which used to consist of an extra moment of eye contact, laughing at a man's jokes, or "accidentally" touching his hand when he handed you something, has taken on a more overt and definitely unpleasant tone, in our estimation. As the article explains, flirting has been elevated to an art form. We are then introduced to Fay, Renee, Mary, Krystal, and Pam. They hail from Newark, Chicago, Houston, and so on.

Renee's tactic for successful flirting is to wear the tightest, most revealing dress in her closet, and then when at the club walk back and forth to the bathroom all night long, showing off her hourglass figure.

Mary describes herself as the queen of the double entendre. She uses the play-on-words tactic, saying to the man she has her eye on things like, "I have a quick wit and a quick tongue." She also might say, "I would love to lick an ice cream cone," letting that tongue linger on the word "lick." Mary flirts with interested mechanics or men who are getting their cars repaired by asking, "What's the matter? Need a lube job?"

Pam loves the crowded bar because it gives her a chance for bodily contact. After she sandwiches her way between a couple of men, she nuzzles against one of them. If done right, she advises, you never have to spend a dime for a drink. She likes to catch men off guard by touching them, their hand, their shoulder, their beard, or caressing their bald head.

The article suggests there are those bold and brash women who'll go so far as to "do the Sharon Stone routine," referring to the infamous *Basic Instinct* scene where Stone gives onlookers either their money's worth or more than they paid for.

Mary points out that a straw and a glass can be great props for flirting. She caresses the glass up and down, up and down, or she puts the straw in her mouth. "Even Ray Charles could see what's on her mind," the article states.

There's the usual suggestion that a guy should slip his business card in a girl's pocket with his home number on the back. Pam say's he's likely to have a message from her on his machine before he even gets home. Finally, Krystal has left the nightclub with bruised knees from rubbing her legs against men in an attempt to get their attention.

I don't mean to imply that Faye and Pam are bitches or hoes, but we are faced here with women who seem desperate, aggressive, and confused about sex and who are sending messages to men they may not ultimately mean. I don't remember flirting being anything like this when I was younger. For my friends and me, a longer glance, a smile, asking for the time—that's about as far as our flirting went. If he didn't pick up on our interest he was either too fast or too slow for us.

Rather than making obvious assumptions about these young women or about what these young men are being taught to look for from women, I'd rather comment on what it has done to my friend and her choices in raising her sons. She is finding herself increasingly alienated from the Black community as she looks for guidance in raising healthy men who happen to be Black. If the magazines are teaching her sons that and the boys in the 'hood are teaching them how to be cool, she is wondering where she should turn for images and social outlets that will help to raise men who have strong self-images based not on sexual conquests or violent confrontations but on personal accomplishments.

I couldn't forget the observation made by one of the girls at North High School, when she pointed out that the girls in her school who are receiving Ds are the ones chasing the boys who want to be drug dealers. I would suspect that the girls receiving Ds also have very few plans for the future, and that the boys know it. These girls are chasing boys, especially the ones who they think will make big money fast, and probably using little more than their sexuality to hook the boys' interest. Could it be that these are the girls who wave their hands in the air and shout, "Yeah, I'm a gangsta bitch"? Are these the girls who are being referred to as bitches and hoes? Are these girls simply victims of the same ghettocentric mentality that has prevailed in the inner cities for almost a decade?

"Can Girls Be Cool?"

Generally, yes. A girl can be cool, as in "cool with me," but most girls aren't *cool* cool. Women are in some ways immune to the dictates of cool. The responsibilities associated with the onset of the menstrual cycle immediately begin to mature a young girl. The possibility of bearing children makes a young girl want and need things that require a more stable existence. So because of nature, a girl matures in a very "American" way—desiring and figuring out how to have more, in the hopes of ensuring stability.

Women are not defined by whether they cry or not. They are not required to fight and win, or to display their mettle. One might argue that the girls of the inner city are under the same pressures and fears as the boys. That is true. And through need they must demonstrate their toughness as well. But that need is simply survival. That need has nothing to do with the need to define her very femaleness. If she is "soft," she will still be a woman. If she runs from a fight or avoids certain situations, her womanness is not destroyed.

It seems that in the streets boys can't just go through puberty and then become men. They must demonstrate their manhood or else be constantly challenged.

Cool seems to dictate a certain level of prowess with the ladies. But in the streets, love is still not a luxury one can afford. Vulnerability is a dangerous thing. Again, love is there, but it's rarely demonstrated in public. And because so many young street girls play so many games with their men, these men learn not to trust them with love and vulnerability.

To the boy who is trying to be cool and who is caught in cool's negative spiral, getting women and proving you got them becomes very important. In the streets, proof often becomes sex, and eventually pregnancy.

"Look What I Did!"

Pregnancy is a badge sometimes. For those who are really desperate to prove their manhood, getting a girl pregnant can be the ultimate. For a hot minute he feels manly, cool. But often the teenage father suddenly realizes he's got a child— and that he is now responsible for that child. If he tackles the responsibilities and he's unprepared (no education, no money, no job), anger surfaces. He's not cool anymore, because he can't run with his buddies. Pressures from the girl and both their families might be intense. If he hasn't matured to the point of harnessing that anger and fear, he could lose it all.

Then there is the young man who rejects the notion of fatherhood and disconnects himself emotionally from his child. He becomes cold—not cool—and he then learns that he can emotionally disconnect from a lot of things.

The girl's responsibility in this unwanted pregnancy is not to be ignored. But it's a very big issue to tackle. Some of the teenage mothers, who are often "good" girls, get pregnant just to get themselves out of the streets, not stopping to think that their actions might end up trapping them further. Unfortunately, there are still too many who are caught up in the culture of cool. She's *having his baby.*

Recently, I was riding my bike in Central Park while enjoying a beautiful Saturday afternoon. The park was filled with people flying kites, riding bikes, Rollerblading, eating hot dogs, sipping spring water. Then I noticed groups of young Black teenage boys riding bikes, laughing and talking. There was a Little League game of young Black boys, and dozens of others were Rollerblading or just hanging out. I suddenly realized something was missing. Where were the young Black girls? They weren't in the park.

I asked a friend later, "What do you think? Where are all the Black girls on such a beautiful day?" "Pregnant," she answered, without hesitation. "I take the subway every day, so I know. I see them hauling these strollers."

I had to think about that for a minute. The young Black teenage boy is in Central Park, free and getting lots of fresh air. The Black girl is home watching the kids. Is she happy? Is she healthy? Is she free of stress? How does she handle those kids, especially the male child who might not have a mature father figure nearby and who might become a product of street cool one day? Does this stressed-out mother contribute to the phenomenon of Black females having become "bitches and hoes"? Does her proclivity to slap, whack, yell, demand, and threaten her child when he misbehaves, or simply spills his juice, have anything to do with the level of anger and violence among Black boys today? Without a doubt.

I feel we have given far too much attention to the young Black male, who has a system he has become comfortable with called *cool* to guide him toward manhood, while the young Black girl is a victim of his cool and of her own desires to have him. What did she envision when she got pregnant? Capturing him? And then what did she envision for their lives? Why are her dreams and her realities so far apart?

Who Is Cool?

I asked the kids at North for some examples of girls who are cool. One name came up, Queen Latifah, because "she stays true to herself." However, one of the girls at North had to make this unfortunate observation: "I like Queen Latifah, but they're trying to say she's a lesbian. They're saying that about Toni Braxton, too. They're always dissing the Black female." ("They" was unspecified.)

This was a very real and important observation. Maybe it's my imagination, but there seems to be a tradition of the famous successful and attractive (although that is not always an essential trait) Black female being stigmatized in some way. For lack of a better term, I call it the "She thinks she's cute" syndrome. This label is such anathema for a Black female that inevitably that person must be made to get back in line. Once a neighbor and I were talking about a girl in the building who was becoming a young lady. She had that confidence that comes with attractiveness, and others in the building had begun whispering, "She thinks she's cute." My neighbor then said, "So what—let her! It's about time cute young Black girls be allowed to know it. Free them from this prison." I had to agree—and go one step further: When she becomes a beautiful woman, don't stigmatize or ostracize her just because of her beauty.

While the girl around the block is becoming a "bitch" or "whore," the highly successful Black woman is being rumored a lesbian or is being called "Diva" by members of the Black community.

"Diva" has become a popular new label for many successful Black women, everyone from Susan L. Taylor of *Essence* magazine to Maya Angelou. This isn't a case of not knowing the meaning of the word, but more a perception that automatically clicks in about glamorous and successful Black ladies. "Diva" conjures up women who are grandiose, exaggerated, almost caricatures of womanhood. It has been so frustrating that I decided to look up the term:

> Diva: A prima donna.
> Prima donna: 1. The leading female soloist in an opera company. 2. A temperamental and conceited performer.

The September '94 issue of *Allure* magazine calls Whoopi Goldberg a "Diva in Dreadlocks." Whoopi, a diva? It doesn't work for me. While successful Black women become *divas*, teenaged Black boys become *youths*. *Youths* conjures up someone with handcuffs on, and when I see a magazine featuring fashion for kids and the caption under the young Black males describes them as *youths* while those below young whites describe them as *teenagers*, I get very suspicious. Thus in this book I've tried to refer to Black *boys* when they are boys and Black *teenagers* when they're in their teens, and so on.

These labels leave young Black girls with no one to look up to, no one real and tangible; they separate and stigmatize the successful and beautiful Black woman.

There are millions of young Black boys/men growing up with the rules of street cool because they are stuck in the inner city and are trying to survive and even conquer it. Again, this boy/man's tools are insufficient for the larger society, but are fine-tuned for his own environment. The young men who survive and are deemed "cool" in this environment will be very different from the kind of "men" America wants them to be.

These young men are also different from those who made it out of the inner city through schoolwork, athletics, strong parental control, and job growth. The young men who escape the streets through more conventional American methods are finding themselves on college campuses.

The seventies brought an influx of young Black folks onto college campuses. They were pioneers. They were the class of Blacks who had previously had no hope of going to college; because prior to the sixties and seventies, it was only the traditional privileged-class Blacks whose children went to college. Because of the civil rights movement and other rebellions, more streetwise Black students were now treated to solid elementary and secondary educations and were subsequently ready for college and beyond.

That was then; this is now. Young Black people attending colleges today have experienced the racist eighties, which stigmatized their enrollment as "reverse discrimination." Opportunities to attend colleges dried up. The government no longer offered student loans to private colleges. Black colleges became very popular. Bill Cosby wore a different college sweatshirt every Thursday night on his TV show, and boasted of attending Hillman College—a thinly veiled disguise of Hampton University in Virginia. Spelman, Howard, and other historically Black universities were the places to be. Enrollment in Black colleges swelled. To some it was great; to others it felt like Jim Crow all over again.

As a result of all this, young Black students who are in private colleges today are well aware that they belong there.

Young Black men who are found on some of these campuses seem to be defining their future selves based on cool's determination to exist. But this is not the cool of the seventies that evolved into success without compromise (although many certainly did compromise). This is a cool defined by the overtly racist, sexist eighties and by the aggressive hip-hop—male-dominated—generation.

I have just returned from a visit to my alma mater, Trinity College in Hartford, Connecticut. This Black alumni weekend was filled with discussion about Trinity's tradition of bringing Black students to the school and then letting them fend for themselves on a hostile campus. The white students at Trinity, although oblivious to their role, are poised and polished gatekeepers to American society. They don't burn crosses, but they impose their racial notions on their Black fellow students as the editors of the campus newspaper or the campus literary magazine.

Their intellectual self-righteousness makes it difficult for Black students to recognize racist overtones.

A panel discussion one day featured several Black alumni, including a recent male graduate. This young man talked about the student government elections of his senior year, 1993. As an example of the level of racism he and his Black classmates had had to deal with, he told us about how white students were heard shouting, "These niggas think they're running the campus" and "No nigga for class president."

The audience sat appalled. However, I fixated on the fact that even though Trinity's student body was actually saying, "These niggas think they're running the campus," this young Black man had managed to become the class president his senior year. I then asked, "Wait a minute, are you telling me you were president of the student body here last year?" Suddenly the audience began applauding his accomplishment. I don't care what the white students were shouting. If anything, it's another example of the *trick* of racism. If we dwell on the use of the word *nigga* and the protest of white students over having a Black student body president, we miss the beauty of his triumph. They can't trick me. I can see the tree in the forest of racism! This young Black man was president of the student body at Trinity in his senior year. That is progress we should not ignore. Whenever white folks start protesting and shouting racist epithets, you know Black folks have just made a great stride somewhere. I say focus on the triumph; let them scream.

While the discussion was in full bloom, I noticed eight male students marching in together. They took seats along the side. Caught up in the discussion, I put it in the back of my mind.

The next day, as I was walking to the parking lot to drive back home, a female student, Pat, stopped me and a fellow alumni. She wanted to talk about her future in writing.

After a while I wanted to talk about the here and now, so I mentioned to her that at a party the night before the young male students hadn't seemed very warm. They were partying hard enough, but they weren't partying with us; they seemed to be separate, remote. This young woman's eyes lit up, her face changed, her smile broadened. "You noticed?" she asked. There was a pleading, begging tone in her voice, almost like, "Please, tell me you noticed." I nodded, "Yeah, I noticed. What's going on?"

Pat explained how the Black girls on campus plan parties, buy new dresses and shoes, do their hair and makeup, and then go to the party—with each other. They never have dates. The men on campus don't ask them out. She quickly explained this incredible division between the Black men and women. The Black men have established an organization on campus, and the Black women have theirs. Also, I noticed one of the male students the night before dancing with two white girls at one time at the Umoja house. What I saw was an emphatic statement that felt somewhat threatening. The men seemed defiant. They seemed to be putting the women in their place by ignoring them. I then asked, "Pat, why don't you and your girlfriends start dating outside the race?"

"We've been thinking about it," she replied. "We had a meeting and said, 'Look, if we don't have dates for the next party, we're going to go ask some other guys.' "

"Pat," I said. "This doesn't have to be an organizational decision, does it? It's important that a young woman feel what it's like to be pursued. It makes her feel pretty, sexy, confident. If the Black guys on campus won't supply that feeling, maybe you should go out with others."

I shuddered. My God, was I Black-male bashing? How could I stand there and talk about dating anyone other than Black men?

Then I looked at Pat. Her face appeared calmer, her smile more genuine. It seemed Pat had fallen into the Black female's habit of developing her career while ignoring an equally important issue, the thing that might make her work at school infinitely easier—that she needed a young man to go to parties with, to enjoy a movie with, to study with. This is when politics becomes personal.

During the drive home I thought about all this. I was angry with all those good-looking Black men I saw at that party for making Pat feel this way. I was angry with my contemporaries, because our generation had been suffering with so much anger and confusion in our relationships that we were not providing any kind of role models for these young men and women. And then I was angry with the generation before me, my parents, because they had set a poor example for me.

After we talked with Pat I talked to Marcia, a fellow alumnus. Marcia told me about her disastrous marriage to her former husband. Marcia said, "One thing Black women aren't doing is talking to their daughters. My mother never told me anything about what to expect from a man, or how to be patient. I do remember her one time saying to me, 'If you can just wait until he's about forty . . .' That was it. She didn't tell me what that meant. All she needed to say to me was, 'Listen Marcia, he loves you, he just isn't ready. Be patient, don't take everything so personally, and eventually he will calm down and be with you.' If she had said that I would have been different. And maybe we would have made it."

That wasn't Black-male bashing. Marcia wasn't talking about how lousy Black men are. She was acknowledging how most men can find adjusting to marriage and maturity a very difficult task—Black men most of all because Black women haven't been schooled about it all yet. (Another reason that growing up is hard for some Black males is that many of them never had a childhood. If life was hard during the earliest years, adulthood becomes a time to be free, to have fun. But that's no excuse, especially if he has brought a new life into the world. It's time to realize that two wrongs don't make a right. Give your child a childhood so that he can become a full-fledged man, ready for adulthood.)

Marcia told me some of the horrors of her marriage. Allan was a quiet, good-looking, well-liked man. He and Marcia were always a couple and their relationship had always been volatile. Still, sometime after college Allan married Marcia, and all anyone ever heard was how bad things were going.

After two kids Allan fell in love with crack. Marcia described the night he broke her nose and she broke her hand trying to stop him from taking their two children out of the house. It was frightening. Marcia then relayed something very significant. Their worst argument had been over three dollars.

Marcia and Allan lived in Washington. Both were graduates of highly respected undergraduate and graduate schools. They were the perfect Black couple, perhaps. One day, Marcia was preparing lunch. She had invited her son's teacher to their home so she could assure herself that the school was taking care of business.

Allan was walking out the door and Marcia asked him for three dollars to get cheese and crackers. The way she explained it to me, Allan's male ego did not allow him to tell her he didn't have it, so instead he simply said, "You're a little social butterfly." Marcia went off. *"Social butterfly"? She's having lunch with their son's teacher so he will get a proper education. And if Allan was a better father and man, he would be sticking around to meet this teacher.* The argument escalated.

Marcia later found out he didn't have the money, and she felt bad that he hadn't been able to tell her that.

There was obviously much more going on. Perhaps Marcia *was* being a social butterfly. This is not uncommon for American women. Most American women, regardless of their color, want to have the elegant life they see on the screen and in magazines. That life includes dinner parties, charm-school table manners, tailored suits for him, elegant dresses for her, and so on.

In the fifties, Black men wanted that too, because it was something they couldn't have before. As explained in the chapter on middle-class cool, that is why there were so many Uncle Toms and Handkerchief Heads, because in order for black men to achieve that life, they had to compromise a great deal of themselves in the workplace.

During the sixties the woman's place in the revolution was "prone," as Stokely so nicely informed us. That pronouncement was a death knell for that feisty, tough, assertive, determined Black woman, who essentially wanted her man to provide a traditional American life for her. Allan may not have had the money, but he also wasn't interested in having tea with the teacher. Lunching was not on his agenda, and he wasn't sure if he wanted a wife with that kind of calendar. Frankly,

Allan didn't know what his agenda was, since previously, the only agenda had been the American agenda.

It was somewhere around the seventies that Black men began to realize that they didn't need that feisty, assertive woman. They had choices. "The darker the berry" was the slogan in the sixties, while the seventies allowed Black men to sample white women in record numbers (white women were releasing a lot of guilt and anger—allowing them to vote conservative, guilt-free, in the eighties).

With the Reagan era, the eighties was a return to the tradition of light-skinned Black women who were perceived to be pretty and refined and seen as better prepared to be a partner to a successful man. Not surprisingly, this was the era of the rise of bitches and hoes. As *he* got paid, *she* got put in her place.

Afrocentricity

There is a growing dichotomy between Black men and women today. And it is no coincidence that the rise in afrocentricity and this dichotomy are occurring at the same time. The assertive, bossy Black woman is slowly becoming a dinosaur. She is obsolete. She has served her purpose. (Yes, I know I'm way out on a brittle limb here.)

In a way, Black Americans had overcome. The battle—if not the war—had finally been won, because Black *men* were somewhat free. Some have said, "The Civil War freed the white man and the Black woman. The white woman and the Black man are still enslaved." If that was at one time true, then the Black revolution and the civil rights movement of the 1960s had finally succeeded in setting some—if not all—Black men free.

Now, it seems, Black men are determined to create the life, family structure, lifestyle, community, movies, activities, and children they have always wanted to create. However it is going to be *their way*. And that means the Black woman will no longer be "in charge." The Black will would have to change or get out of the way.

If you notice, once you've had power, it's very difficult—nearly impossible—to relinquish it, as proved by white American men. Well, the Black woman has enjoyed some power for a long time. And she is not willing, nor is she prepared, to let it go. Because in part she doesn't even know that she has had it.

He knows, however. He is no longer interested in having her hold on to very much power. It's refreshing in a way that young Black men are saying, *That's it, I'm going to do it my way*. It's exciting that he can finally do that. Afrocentricity and ghettocentricity are his way of declaring that to the nation. He will not make the skin-trade. He will succeed and establish a community on *his* terms. Essentially, he will stay with what's comfortable. If it's not comfortable, he will move on. Being "white"—whatever that means to him—is not comfortable. So enter afrocentricity.

In order for him to establish his own community, he must finally be the head of his family. His head must stay clear, his goals must be the family's goals; for his family's social mobility will be determined mostly by what *he* is able to accomplish. If his wife is a professional woman, her money and talents should enhance what he is achieving.

It's an exciting time for Black men. Cool is finally achieving its fullest potential. While in the previous chapter I make the case for cool's obsolescence, I am contradicting myself here by saying that the struggles between Black men and Black women reflect the Black male's uncompromising decision to be himself, to be cool.

There are many women who would say, *No, the problem is that he has no more excuses. Society is giving him jobs, his money is accepted on the stock exchange just like everyone else's money—he just doesn't want to get a job, get busy, pay the price.*

Then there are others who recognize that many Black men identify deeply with those on the corner, the ones who were left behind, who were disenfranchised when the doors closed in the late seventies. That tug makes them angry and confused, and often brings their climb to a halt.

And still, there are those who recognize that the Black male is like any other male. He needs a posse. He needs his male friends around him in order to feel strong. After all, white men have America, they have the military and the police, they have the infrastructure. Black men would love to have Africa, but life is too short to wait that long. So they have an urgent need to stay where they are until they can leave en masse with their brothers. There is strength in numbers. And so, afrocentricity gives them a good excuse to stay culturally correct, to stay where they are comfortable (as most American men like to do), *to stay put.*

But it is deeper than that, because there are those brothers at Trinity. They have no interest in staying put, and they're not afraid to get a job, and they actually *have* a posse that's big enough to help them through. These young men are putting their collective foot down. They will have their own families, and in their own time, and of their own design. End of discussion.

This could be a beautiful thing. But it isn't. What's really a drag about it is that the determined, independent, outspoken, occasionally sharp-tongued, confident, Black woman who has been reluctantly responsible for keeping things going, and who is proud of that fact, is now a dinosaur.

Isiah Thomas's mother is now famous for having fought the evils of the inner city to help ensure that her children thrived. Forgive me, Ms. Thomas, if I have the details wrong, since even if I am, the scenario can be applied to thousands of Black American families. Did she raise a shotgun at someone to protect her kids so that Isiah would grow up to have a family of his own in which he felt he had to take a backseat to his wife? Did she do it so that he would come out and feel so threatened by American society that he would hold himself back on the court, have a short basketball career, crawl into a bottle, and beat his wife and kids? I don't think so. And neither does Isiah. Mrs. Thomas did it so that her son would succeed; and make enough money to provide for his family and be the head of his family (whatever that means within the four walls of his home).

But what of Isiah's sisters if he has sisters? What did they see and learn? Was it how to be strong, how to protect, to figure things out, to strive, to commit, to fight, *to win*? They learned how to kick ass when necessary, they learned that you don't need a man to make it because you can make it on your own, just like your mother did. They learned that you will always *want* a good man, but he's hard to find. They learned that he might even disappear, or might need guidance, love, and pa-tience, and that when all is said and done, *you* still might have to leave *him. But you're a Black woman and you're strong, And you can make it. You can be whoever you want to be, just like my boy Isiah.*

I don't know Isiah's sisters, nor do I know how they have fared in life. But I do know Pat. She grew up in the South Bronx, in the projects. Her mother (she didn't talk about her father) is worried that she isn't taking classes in something she can get a job in. Her mother isn't talking to her about the young men on campus and how to snag one. She's teaching her how to make it out there on her own.

Using these sisters of Isiah's as an illustration, the Black woman who is self-sufficient and eager to achieve might have become impatient with a Black man with a different agenda, as did the young woman at North High School who had decided to date out of the race. *If* the Black woman redefines her goals in a more afrocentric or ghettocentric way, which many have done—not to get a man but because she too sees the fallacies and inequities in the American system and has chosen to lead a more culturally aware and balanced life—she and he might be on the same path. If she is seeking the good life, American style, her choices of a Black male partner are becoming increasingly limited and she is becoming increasingly frustrated. A woman, Black or white—a person, Black or white—should have the opportunity to make a choice and still lead a satisfying life filled with a family and fulfilling and meaningful work.

Today's young Isiahs (with less basketball skills, to be sure) are learning to make it on their own, with the support of both parents. They are envisioning a life where they are comfortable. If that comfort means staying within the confines of the Black community in their heads and in their souls, that's the way it will be.

That is the reality. And that is why Pat is suffering She is not what the Black man needs in order to build his domain, because he no longer needs anyone in order to do that. He plans to select a woman he *wants*, and his criteria are very different from that of his father and grandfather.

The nineties are seeing the decade of the dinosaur—that feisty, strong, hardworking Black woman who is determined to achieve the American dream of success and who has had to drag her man along and teach him the ways of the world (or so she felt, or so he felt, or so it appeared)—and the rise of the young Black male as a self-defined entity. It's scary and exciting at the same time.

Epilogue

was recently riding the New York City subway on my way to an appointment in midtown. It was an express train, so passengers were in close quarters for relatively long stretches of time. At the 72nd Street stop, two Black men entered my car. Both of them carried three huge bags of snacks—popcorn, tortilla chips, potato chips, whatever—and they sat across from me on a completely empty bench, threw down their bags, and, taking up half the bench, started talking.

"Alvin, man, you won't believe what I had to do last night. Man, my mother called me and told me to get down there. Vicki was going off, man. So I hops on the train and get to my mom's. Man, Vicki was steamin'. She was cursin' and fumin' and talkin' about how she was goin' out to kick TJ's ass. Man, she was serious, too. She was gonna leave the house and go to TJ's block and kick his ass."

"Yeah, man?"

"Yeah. I had to push her down on the bed, man. I told her, I said, 'Look, Vicki, just calm yo' ass down. You ain't goin' nowhere. You gonna stay right here till you calm yo'self down."

"Yeah, man?"

"Yeah. She stood right back up, and she was all hysterical and callin' me a mothafucka and all that shit, and tellin' me to get out her way. She was really gonna do it, man. She was gonna go

195

over to TJ's and try to fight him. Finally, man, I just stood in the doorway and put my arms up and blocked her path, man. I just stood there, man, and told her she wasn't goin' nowhere, and she betta calm down."

"Did she, man?"

"Finally, man, she sat down on the bed cursin' and yellin' at everybody. But she calmed down. My other sister and my mother was yellin' and screamin' behind me the whole time. Man, it was crazy. What did she think she was gonna do to TJ? That man mighta kicked her ass or blowed her away."

"I don't know, Bobby, Vicki a strong girl, I bet."

Then they both cracked up. These two guys were in their early thirties, wearing the usual sneakers, jeans, T-shirts, and hats (turned the correct way; backwards is for shorties, aka kids). I was so fascinated I was staring, and Alvin noticed. Bobby, who was the better-looking of the two, turned to me and smiled. I tried to look away to pretend I wasn't dead in their business, but it was too late. I knew they could give me some flak for not minding my own business. Instead I noticed Alvin pass Bobby his pen and a slip of paper.

"How you doin' today?" Bobby said to me.

"Fine," I answered politely.

"You goin' to work? Oh, it's kind of late, you goin' to lunch or somethin'?"

"To a meeting."

"Maybe you'd like to have lunch with me sometime," he said. I noticed he was ready to write my phone number on the paper Alvin had slipped him. I begged off, and Bobby smiled a somewhat toothless smile and said he understood. When the doors opened and I stood up he bid me a nice day.

This scene is memorable because Bobby's story to Alvin demonstrated something that is important to think about. Bobby's mother called him to come down to her house to handle this situation. His sister was out of control and was going into the streets to fight a grown man. Their mother was at her wit's end, and her solution was to phone Bobby. Bobby came and handled the situation, and he succeeded. It might not have been just his physical strength that subdued Vicki, but also his calm head and his genuine concern for her welfare.

Bobby is a mature man in some ways. But these are the kinds of problems he has to deal with on a daily basis. Do we expect Bobby to dress in a suit the next day and go to a desk job, buy a little house in the suburbs, and open up a 401-K? Is that what Bobby *needs* to do in order to help his family out? Is it realistic for us to think Bobby will even be capable of doing that one day, any day, at any time in his lifetime? Is it fair, though, not to respect Bobby as a man because he might never have the 401-K? What about his level head, his willingness to help his mother and family when called upon, his caring for his sister?

Is it Bobby's fault he's uneducated? Is it his fault he doesn't have much of a job? Is Bobby not being a man in the context of his environment?

When I first began this book, I was singing the praises of cool. I was young and revolutionary and thought white people were the enemy. Cool was a triumph of spirit, a rational reaction to an irrational situation. As I matured, cool got in the way.

I grew up in New York City's Central Harlem, eventually moving to Morningside Heights. When I was placed in a white elementary public school in the "Silk Stocking District" of New York City, I danced to James Brown *and* the Beatles. I grew up attending Riverside Church, a haven of interdenominational faiths and a completely integrated congregation with white people who truly seemed to be fair, and who were fighting very hard for racial equality and justice in America. It was utopia. But I didn't know that. I thought this was the way the world was.

I was rudely awakened, not just by my college years—which were filled with revolutionary Blacks (including myself, because the late sixties made me increasingly aware of the injustices of racism) and whites from sheltered families, who made stupid and racist remarks and behaved like the gatekeepers they are—but also by the renewed racism of the eighties, when liberals were kicked in the groin, idealism was the reason for drugs and long hair, and when a real attempt was made to reverse all that had been achieved for Black America during the previous two decades. I was stunned, numb. I truly, honestly, and wholeheartedly believed, and still do, in the family of man. Race is a smoke screen and a handy way to manipulate whole groups of people, to get them to focus elsewhere, anywhere other than where the real problems lie.

Racism affects my life in ways I cannot measure, but it doesn't affect *me*. It doesn't hurt or confuse me; it doesn't make me feel small or inferior. I played with young white kids and slept over at their houses, and they spent the night at mine. They are no different from me.

On my first day at PS 6, the white public school I began attending in fourth grade, my dad stood at the locked classroom door with me, waiting for it to be opened. Several white kids and their parents stood there with us and talked about their summer in Germany or the Hamptons. I had summered on our farm in Oak City, North Carolina, a hundred or so acres of beautiful land, so it never occurred to me that they had gone somewhere that was in any way *better*. When I sat down at my desk, my dad turned to leave. I was the only Black kid in the classroom and I didn't know anyone. When he got to the door, my dad turned back around and walked toward me. He dug in his pocket and pulled out all the change he had and handed it to me.

"Here, take this. This is the only difference between you and them," he said.

It was more change than I'd ever had at one time, and I was delighted. For some reason, I never forgot what he said, even though it didn't mean much at the time.

That's *cool* to me. That's what cool is. My father never allowed in us a sense of inferiority, even though he had suffered injustices. He never hated white people or felt inferior to them. He didn't fear them either. He *got it*. Those coins were the only difference.

It's not about "getting paid." That doesn't make you a man. You *are* a man. It's about a country determined not to pay you, and determined to define what a man is in such a way as to deprive you of that title.

Because I grew up with the Beatles *and* James Brown, because so many white people at Riverside Church and Columbia Grammar and Preparatory School helped me understand things in the same way they helped the white kids understand things, and because I believe in the family of man and do not see racism as an obstacle, I am not considered cool. I'm not angry enough, I'm not revolutionary enough, I'm not "Black" enough. Being cool, and being Black as defined by racial bullies, has sometimes gotten in the way of me being myself. I am a Black woman, immensely proud. And I am proud of Black men. But as they embark on defining themselves more and more in terms of their Blackness, and their cool, they limit their possibilities.

So while being cool has been a triumph of spirit, it is now becoming a mandate, and a means of defining one another in very narrow terms. There is room for all kinds of men, of all colors and hues, all background and ambitions.

A friend once said to me, "This is a problem that gets perpetuated at the urinals." In other words, it's a problem between Black men and white men. There has to be some kind of mutual respect or this war will never end.

Cool is about becoming a man. Becoming a man is about succeeding by the dictates of your environment. It would be very, very cool, and fitting, if America would recognize Black men as the *men* they already are, and begin to support and respect what they have already achieved, because America has the potential to be that great. With self-respect and the respect of his peers (America itself), a man can concentrate on schoolwork, he can concentrate on his relationships with people, he can be all that he can be, because he isn't trying desperately to simply be *somebody.*

I haven't written this book to define cool, to be the arbiter of what is cool and what isn't, or to explain why Black men are the way they are or how white America is to blame for everything that has happened to Black Americans. I hope this book serves the purpose of explaining the phenomenon of cool so that everyone will stop thinking it's a silly, unimportant style of dressing and behaving, without rhyme or reason.

Cool is determined by your peer group, your family, your point of view and perspective. If I tell you I think Bryant Gumbel is cool and you think Dr. Dre is, we invalidate each other. So, I am not here to tell you who or what is cool.

What Is Cool? hopes to tell you that cool is a black boy's way of becoming a man in his environment, with the requisite and well-deserved self-esteem and respect that comes with manhood.